PRACTICAL SECRETARY'S MANUAL AND GUIDE

Yvonne Lovely

PARKER PUBLISHING COMPANY, INC.   WEST NYACK, N.Y.

© 1978 *by*

Parker Publishing Company, Inc.

West Nyack, New York

Library of Congress Cataloging in Publication Data

Lovely, Yvonne,
    Practical secretary's manual and guide.

    Includes index.
    1. Secretaries--Handbooks, manuals, etc.
2. Office practice--Handbooks, manuals, etc.
I. Title.
HF5547.5.L68   651'.3741   78-1958
ISBN 0-13-693804-3

Printed in the United States of America

HOW TO USE
"PRACTICAL SECRETARY'S
MANUAL AND GUIDE"

This book has been written for secretaries who are always searching for more effective ways to improve their secretarial performance. Since it contains information not normally found in other secretarial publications, it will be a valuable addition to the reference books you are now using.

The emphasis is not only on how to perform a wide variety of secretarial tasks and functions, but more important, how to perform them more efficiently and in a way that will draw the greatest cooperation and support from superiors, peers and subordinates. You will find an extraordinary range of practical suggestions for increasing your productivity. For example, the ability to deal effectively with other people is recognized as one of the most important attributes of a successful secretary. This book provides you with specific guidelines for working more productively with people at all levels, not only with those who are cooperative in their interaction with others—but with those who at times can be particularly difficult.

There are also detailed instructions on how to proceed from typing the executive's dictated correspondence—to composing and typing, on your own initiative, letters for his signature which will read as though he dictated them. As another example, you will be given new ways to assume much of the responsibility for arranging meetings for your executive—including what to do and when, even handling inevitable last minute problems that cause some of the best plans to go awry. You will acquire efficient ways to handle travel arrangements from start to finish, including ways to manage the office in the supervisor's absence.

To progress in this important field, all experienced secretaries know they must become a vital part of the executive-secretary team. This book provides you with detailed techniques enabling you to work more successfully with an executive who is responsive to the team concept—as well as working as effectively as possible with a supervisor who is not. For these special cases, there are suggestions for coping with the executive who possesses characteristics which make him particularly difficult to serve. Whenever you feel you are under-utilized in your present position you will discover this book can be particularly helpful. All secretaries will find ideas and suggestions that show ways to progress to a consistently high level of perfor- mance and capability. If you want a broad range of tested, successful ways to more fully realize your own potential in this important profession, this book has been written for *you*.

As a desk manual, it provides a ready reference for ways to improve secretarial skills, along with a broad range of ideas to increase your daily productivity. There are also specific suggestions for organizing your work so you will be able not only to do what is routinely required, but will have time to develop new, more productive ideas that will increase your effectiveness. Identify the section dealing with office responsibilities of greatest concern to you at a given moment, and check the subtitles for specific suggestions; for example, *How to set up and type a report* (Chapter 4).

Note that this book is intended as a manual for quick reference, and a *guide* for the *practical* secretary. The various illustrations can be easily adapted to fit your own particular needs. For example, as a practical secretary, you will find it easy to eliminate some of the headings suggested for a mail register in Chapter 2 (if you decide you need one) and insert those applicable to your own purpose.

The principles of good secretaryship apply no matter where or what the job. If you use the suggestions and guidelines detailed in this book, and blend these ideas with the necessary desire and ambition, you will become a far more successful secretary—and an indispensable asset to your employer.

Yvonne Lovely

CONTENTS

9

Keeping up with an advancing technology ● Keeping
up to date with the latest in office machinery and
supplies ● Your new typewriter—a problem of
selection ● How to type 150 words a minute without
touching the keyboard ● How to select the most
efficient reproduction method and equipment for the job
at hand ● Cooperate with automated equipment, and
it will cooperate with you ● Getting ready for
conversion to the metric system

Creating the proper impression through business
correspondence ● Suggested letter styles ● How to
help your executive prepare his correspondence ●
When and how to correct grammatical errors ● Your
responsibility for papers prepared by others for your
executive's signature

How to plan your work to keep on schedule ● Why
every good secretary should be a clock-watcher ● How
to assign your own priorities ● How to remember to
keep your promises ● How to plan ahead to meet
deadlines on time ● How being well organized will
assure smooth-running conferences and meetings ●
How to use the time you save by being well organized

How to budget time and money ● Saving time by
designing your own forms and rubber stamps ● How
to time-and-motion study your office for greater
efficiency ● The proper way to throw away paper ●
How and when to use telecommunications ● Saving

Chapter 1

HANDLING TELEPHONE CALLS PROPERLY

THE TELEPHONE IS A WONDERFUL INVEN-
TION. Although there are times when a secretary thinks she
would be happy never to hear another ring in the office, we just
can't afford to be without a telephone. Since we must live with
it, we must learn to make proper use of it.

How to answer a telephone efficiently

An office telephone can be answered in a variety of
ways, from a simple "hello" to a lengthy identification which will
cost a long-distance caller more than pennies (for example, "The
International Corporation for Assembling Machinery for Heavy
Construction, Purchasing Division, Requisitions Department,
Ms. Jones speaking"). There is a happy medium somewhere
between an answer with no information and one with too much,
but the identification you use to answer your office telephone
depends upon what your executive wants.

Once you have identified your number or extension to
a degree which will enable the caller to determine that he has

reached the proper telephone, the next step is up to him. Hopefully he will identify himself, state his interest—either to talk to you or to your executive—or ask his question. In any case, remembering that time is money, you should answer his inquiry in the fewest words possible. When the telephone rings, be sure you have pencil and paper at hand; nothing is more irritating to a caller than being asked to "wait a minute while I get a pencil and paper." Make notes from the time the caller speaks—the message, the date, the time, and the name of the caller. If he has not given his name at the beginning of the call, extract it from him before the call is terminated, and if the message appears to require a return call, be sure to get the proper telephone number also. Even if you tear up the note the minute he hangs up, with his question answered, making such a record of each telephone call as a part of your normal routine will be well worth the effort.

You should give your undivided attention to the caller, therefore you should not try to attend to something else while you are conversing with him. If you decide at the end of the conversation that you should have made notes and didn't, you must either irritate the caller by asking him to repeat the information he has just given you, or risk error in trying to remember and record what was said after the conversation has terminated. The latter alternative is more difficult if you are interrupted in recording your notes by another call or by a visitor to the office.

When you are taking a call to be returned later, be sure you have the name and affiliation of the caller and the telephone number. Repeat it to be sure you have recorded it correctly: "Mr. R. B. Jones, Sales Manager of the International Paper Company, telephone 976-4215. I'll ask Mr. X to return your call." You may have the name and number in your files, but check the information anyway. Names of heads of departments, names of companies, company affiliations, and telephone numbers are subject to change from one day to the next.

Give only enough information to the caller to serve the immediate purpose, and no more. "Mr. X is not in the office; may I ask him to return your call?" "I expect him this afternoon (or on Monday, or the first of the month)." Do not include any information concerning where he is or what he is doing. You can never be sure when such additional information will be detrimental to the best interests of the company. "He's attending a meeting in Chicago concerning the XYZ contract" may be just enough of a clue for a competitor to obtain business that would otherwise have come to your company.

And be sure you know to whom you are speaking. For example, your executive's superior might ask, and should be told, where Mr. X is and what he is doing. A good secretary knows who should be told what and how much.

Proper telephone manner and manners

Manner is even more important in a telephone conversation than it is in a person. Be pleasant, friendly, helpful if you can, and honest. "I believe you want data that can be obtained from our Sales Department. If you will call Mr. X at (telephone number) I believe he can help you." "I don't have that information, but I'll be glad to find out who could supply it and ask someone else to call you about the matter." "I'm very sorry that I can't help you. You will want to talk with someone in our Shipping Department—if you will hold a moment, I'll have your call transferred to another number." One can be overly helpful and overstep the bounds of her authority. If you are in the Sales Department, don't try to answer questions concerning a problem in shipping or purchasing. Your "best guess" won't help the caller—let him talk to the person or department responsible for answering his question authoritatively.

When you are taking a call for your executive, a proper question is "May I ask him to return your call, or may I take a message?" Don't say "May I have him (or tell him to) return your call—this implies that you will order your executive to return the call and that he will do so immediately. You do not "order" your executive to do anything, and if he chooses not to return a call after you have given him the message, you have no further responsibility.

Manners are something else, and don't forget them.

"Please," "thank you," and in response to a "thank you," "you're welcome," or "it was a pleasure to be able to help." A pleasant phrase to terminate a conversation can be used in lieu of the standard "good-bye." "Have a good day," or "Have a nice weekend." Don't turn off a caller who says "thank you" sincerely with an efficient but brusque "good-bye."

Be pleasant when you answer the telephone, even if you have threatened, after answering multiple calls in the last few minutes, to uproot the thing by its cable. A person telephoning has a right to expect a pleasant greeting over the impersonal instrument, and a calm unhurried response will soothe the irritated customer with a complaint, continue the rapport with one who is calling to provide a bit of information which is of importance to your office, or establish an impression of willing helpfulness for one who is uncertain that he has called the right office and is looking for advice and assistance.

Hanging up is another operation with the telephone which is not always given the proper attention. Do you replace the telephone in its cradle gently after a suitable interval from the last comment by either yourself or the caller? Remember that if you impatiently place a finger on the disconnect lever immediately after you consider the conversation terminated, the effect is "good-bye". . . .(nothing). If you throw the telephone into its cradle, the person on the other end of the line gets the effect of a dynamite blast in his eardrum. Even if you disconnect to answer another ringing telephone, wait a second or so until the other party has time to take the telephone from his ear before you push the button.

In a business office where there is only one line, the problem of a telephone interruption does not arise. A ringing telephone demands action. The executive breaks off his dictation; a visitor automatically assumes second priority; the secretary stops whatever she is doing and answers the telephone, preferably after the first ring, but no later than after the second. In many business offices today, the problem of answering the telephone is compounded by two or more lines, each ring demanding instant attention; and therein lie many problems for the secretary.

If you are talking on one line and another rings, excuse yourself to the other party and acknowledge the second call. Depending upon the nature of the first call, the second can be acknowledged with the usual identification and a word of explanation. If your first call is near completion, an appropriate remark may be "Mr. Smith's office; will you hold one moment, please?" But not more than "one moment." Terminate the first call as rapidly but as pleasantly as possible—"Please give me your telephone number and I'll ask Mr. Smith to call when he returns to the office . . . Thank you." Then return to the second call; "I'm sorry to have kept you waiting. May I help you?"

In another situation, the first call may be a long-distance call and you are taking some important information in shorthand for your executive. Your answer to the second call may be "Mr. Smith's office . . ." If the call is for your executive and you can put the call through at once, do so and then return to your own call. However, if the second call is anything else, perhaps one you should take care of, simply explain: "May I have your number and return your call in a few minutes? I'm on long distance on the other line."

When there are a number of lines into your office, the problem is more complicated, and particularly so if there are a number of other people who can be reached through your telephone. Handling six calls at once can be nerve-wracking, but with a little practice it can be done, provided you maintain your aplomb. Proper handling of the telephone requires that no line rings more than twice before it is answered, and no one caller is left with a dead telephone any longer than absolutely necessary.

The telephone has its own frustrations for the caller. One guaranteed irritant is a constant busy signal in response to several dials over a period of time. Equally frustrating to the caller is to get no answer in several efforts to reach your office. Depending upon the nature of the call, you can expect at least a part of the time to get an annoyed "I've tried to get Smith all morning, but your line's been busy." Or, "Where is everybody? I've tried to call all afternoon and no answer." There are bound to be days like that. Smooth oil on the troubled waters churning for your executive with something like "I'm very sorry, but this has been a particularly busy morning for Mr. Smith. I believe he can speak with you now if you like." Or, "Mr. Smith was chairing a meeting this afternoon and I was with him to take the minutes. I'm sorry we weren't able to have someone cover our telephones."

Which is worse—having your telephone ring unanswered or having a call to your office answered with a busy signal? An argument in favor of the busy signal is that when a telephone rings and there is no answer, the caller has no way of knowing whether you're out of the office for a few moments or all day. The busy signal is more encouraging; it indicates that someone is probably there and using the telephone. The caller is therefore encouraged to try again later. Some executives don't like to answer a telephone and don't like to hear it ring unanswered. One solution is to have another secretary "cover" your telephone when you're out of the office. If this is not possible, your executive may prefer that you put your lines on hold when you leave.

Learn to be an expert at manipulating your hold buttons. A shining example of caller frustration is: You have obtained the necessary information to determine that the call should be put through to Mr. Smith, so you say "One moment, please . . ." and put the caller on hold. He holds, and holds, and holds, impatience increasing by the second, and imagination running away with him. Is Smith arguing about whether he should take the call? Is Smith just letting him cool his heels? Are you on the other line gossiping with one of the other secretaries, or did you simply put him on hold and go out to lunch? Rather than leave the caller with a dead line for more than a few seconds, go back to the line at intervals or explain at once that you can't put the call through. "Mr. Smith will be with you in a moment; a client is just leaving the office." Or, "I'm sorry, Mr. Smith is on another line; would you like to hold, or shall I ask him to call back?"

Be as alert to help your fellow secretary when you're talking with her over the telephone as you expect her to be willing to help you. When you hear another telephone ring in her office while you are speaking, interrupt yourself to ask "Do you have to catch the other phone?" She will be as grateful as you would be for the same courtesy. If you are speaking and your own telephone rings, interrupt yourself with an "Excuse me while I answer the other line." The problem is more difficult if the other party is talking and another line in your office begins to ring. If the other party is a secretary who is not as considerate as you would be and keeps on talking, feel free to interrupt her with a "one moment please" and answer the other line. A more delicate situation occurs when the other party is a customer or client who keeps talking while you have another line ringing. Do *not* interrupt until there is a slight pause in what he is saying; then say "Pardon me, please, I'll be back with you in a moment;" but make sure you *are* back "in a moment."

A courtesy which would eliminate many telephone problems if adopted universally is one of identification. You answer your telephone the way your executive directs. You have no identification problem if you answer with "Mr. Smith's office, Ms. Jones speaking." However, if you do not give your name, you should do so if the opportunity arises. "I'm sorry, he isn't in. This is his secretary, Ms. Jones. May I help you?"

When you initiate a call, identify yourself immediately. The way you identify yourself will depend upon the person on the other end of the line. To a secretary well known to you, "This is Alice" may be sufficient. To one less well known, "This is Alice Jones" would be required. To one completely unknown, you may need complete identification, such as "This is Alice Jones, secretary to Mr. Horace Smith of the Acme Construction Company." If you are calling a customer or client on behalf of your own executive, the latter identification is preferable unless you are personally known to the one you are calling.

Thank heavens nobody calls with "Guess who this is?" anymore in so many words, but there are plenty of people who play the game without the words. "Hello, Ms. Jones, did you get that information I sent to you last week?" You try to identify the voice, running through what "information" he could be talking about that has reached your office sometime during the past five or six hectic working days, and finally give up. Rather than frankly ask "Who is this?", you try a more polite way to learn his name. You may ask, "Is this Mr. Bettis?" even if you don't know any Mr. Bettis. Of course, he may say "No, guess again!" But you can hope that he will reply with his own name, then perhaps you will have a clue concerning the information he has sent you.

How and when to screen telephone calls

The trend in recent years has been for the executive to place his own calls. In most cases, this is a time-saving measure as well as a money-saving one, particularly if he also answers his own telephone. An exception is if a call is to be made on a special telephone system or through a number of switchboards; in this case, it is more efficient for a secretary to place the call. (Presumably the executive's time is worth more to the company than the secretary's.) It should be remembered, however, that the executive's wish is the secretary's command, and if he demands that she screen his calls to determine in advance who is calling and for what, then she does just that.

There is no problem if the caller identifies himself at once; but if he doesn't, how does the secretary extract this information? A standard question is "May I tell him who is calling?" This is perhaps the least irritating of the many ways the question could be phrased. Never say "Who's calling?" If the voice is from the blue, "May I tell him who is calling?" is not likely to be resented, but a good secretary will learn to recognize the voices of those who call frequently; in fact, she will make it her business to recognize the voices so that she can say, in response to "May I speak to him?", "Yes, Mr. Jordan, one moment, please," all the while buzzing the intercom or otherwise making an attempt to connect the caller with her executive so that the time required to put the caller in communication with the executive is minimized.

When a caller asks "May I speak to him, please?" suppose the secretary replies "Mr. Allen?" and he says "No, this is Mr. Blumberg of the Atlas Equipment Company." The secretary need say only "I'm sorry, Mr. Blumberg, one moment please," and she doesn't have to ask his name and company affiliation. On the other hand, if it *is* Mr. Allen, he's pleased that she recognized his voice.

Time is our most precious commodity. We know that not only years are important, but in business, hours, minutes, and even seconds are not to be wasted. Call a number looking for Mr. Johnson, and he answers the telephone. Instant success! Next best: The secretary answers, "One moment please" and there is Mr. Johnson. Being friendly, cheerful, and pleasant is necessary, but even these qualities can be carried to the extreme. The secretary answers, but with "Yes, uh, huh, of course you may, just one moment please. . . ." and then the hold button. A waste of words and time.

How to give or take a message by telephone

This section is included because it is so obviously necessary. There *are* secretaries who don't know how to give or take a message by telephone. First, *always be sure to identify yourself*, especially if you are giving a message.

When you make a call, be sure you include the information you would want if you were taking the message. *Example:* You call, "Is he there?" You have no complaint if his secretary says "yes" and hangs up. If that is really your question, you have your answer. Better,—"Is he there? Mr. Smith would like to come down for a few minutes."

In another situation, your question should properly be "Mr. Smith would like to speak with Mr. Jones. Is he there?" Suppose he isn't, or he isn't available to talk at that moment. Then ask to have the call returned, but not by an "ask him to call us." If you call often, she may know you, your executive and your number; if you do *not* call often, or if she is a substitute for the regular secretary, she is not a mind reader. Give her the information she needs: "Ask him to call Mr. Smith of the Atlas Construction Company, telephone 926-7843. It's about the contract with Roberts Realty."

When your telephone rings, remove the telephone from the cradle and at the same time pick up a pencil—and be sure you have note paper at hand. If there is a message to be taken, take it—in shorthand, or longhand, and be sure to get the name with proper spelling if you don't recognize it immediately, and ask for the telephone number. If you know the name and assume you know the telephone number, simply ask, "Yes, Mr. Blumberg, and your number is 862-9748?" *Never* give your executive a telephone call to return with no notation other than "Call Mr. Blumberg." Your executive has enough on his mind—be considerate enough to save him the trouble of looking up the number or asking you to do it for him. He should have to do neither.

Once you have taken a message for your executive and given it to him, your responsibility is discharged—provided you make sure he has at least observed that the message is there. In some cases, you will want to provide a spindle to skewer the messages on as they come in; a good substitute for a spindle is a desk pen—he can't ignore a message that is flagrantly under his nose. Just be sure a message is not buried in other paper on his desk.

Your executive will determine in what order, or if, he returns his calls. A junior executive once frankly admitted he was completely undemocratic when it came to returning his telephone calls: "I return them in order directly proportional to the caller's position on the organization chart." That's his business.

In addition to giving or taking telephone messages, your executive may want you to keep a running record of *all* incoming and outgoing calls. Depending upon his needs, you may find it helpful to set up a sheet for each day in a bound notebook of the appropriate size to record the information desired. Record the name of the person and the number, the result (completed or "will call," including the date the call is expected to be returned), and possibly the subject of the call. This is helpful as a check on which calls have not yet been completed, as well as a reminder that a report promised on the 17th has not yet been received (or sent, as the case may be).

Long-distance calls

In many cases there is no substitute for a personal conversation between two people, regardless of the cost involved to arrange it. Important conversations should always be confirmed in writing, but your executive is the one to determine when a long-distance call is to be made.

When the call is made within your own time zone, assuming both offices have the same hours of business, a long-distance call can be made with the same consideration as local calls; that is, a call around noon is quite likely to find that the person wanted is out to lunch. When, however, the called party is in a different time zone, there may be the problem that office hours are not the same because of the time differential. For example, even though hours are 9:00 a.m. to 5:30 p.m. in offices in New York, Chicago, Denver, and San Francisco, and you are in New York, the "open" hours for your telephone contacts are as follows: Chicago, 10:00 to 5:30; Denver, 11:00 to 5:30, and San Francisco, 12:00 to 5:30.

When your call is made overseas, the problem is compounded. In addition to the time differential, there is the International Date Line to be considered, as well as the practice in many foreign countries of extended lunch periods. If you make overseas calls regularly, you will soon learn the best time to call each office, wherever it is.

How to tell what time it is anywhere
else in the world

The basis for standard time throughout most of the world is Greenwich Mean Time (GMT). Standard time zones are indicated in tables found in reference books, such as airline guides and secretarial handbooks, as ± the number of hours difference from GMT. The chart in Figure 1 will help you determine what time it is anywhere else in the world; simply select

Nome	Honolulu, Anchorage	Whitehorse	San Francisco (PST) Vancouver, Juneau	Denver (MST) Salt Lake City	Chicago (CST) Winnipeg, Mexico City	New York (EST) Montreal	San Juan, Halifax, Santiago	Buenos Aires, Rio de Janeiro	Cape Verde	Azores	London (GMT)	Berlin, Brussels, Paris, Madrid, Rome, Amsterdam, Stockholm	Athens, Capetown, Istanbul	Bagdad, Moscow	Bahrain I.	Karachi	Dacca	Bangkok, Manila	Hong Kong, Peking, Shanghai	Tokyo	Melbourne, Sydney, Shanghai	Ponepi, C.I.	Auckland, Wellington
−11	−10	− 9	− 8	− 7	− 6	− 5	4	− 3	− 2	− 1	0	+ 1	+ 2	+ 3	+ 4	+ 5	+ 6	+ 7	+ 8	+ 9	+10	+11	+12
100	200	300	400	500	600	700	800	900	1000	1100	1200	1300	1400	1500	1600	1700	1800	1900	2000	2100	2200	2300	2400
200	300	400	500	600	700	800	900	1000	1100	1200	1300	1400	1500	1600	1700	1800	1900	2000	2100	2200	2300	2400	100
300	400	500	600	700	800	900	1000	1100	1200	1300	1400	1500	1600	1700	1800	1900	2000	2100	2200	2300	2400	100	200
400	500	600	700	800	900	1000	1100	1200	1300	1400	1500	1600	1700	1800	1900	2000	2100	2200	2300	2400	100	200	300
500	600	700	800	900	1000	1100	1200	1300	1400	1500	1600	1700	1800	1900	2000	2100	2200	2300	2400	100	200	300	400
600	700	800	900	1000	1100	1200	1300	1400	1500	1600	1700	1800	1900	2000	2100	2200	2300	2400	100	200	300	400	500
700	800	900	1000	1100	1200	1300	1400	1500	1600	1700	1800	1900	2000	2100	2200	2300	2400	100	200	300	400	500	600
800	900	1000	1100	1200	1300	1400	1500	1600	1700	1800	1900	2000	2100	2200	2300	2400	100	200	300	400	500	600	700
900	1000	1100	1200	1300	1400	1500	1600	1700	1800	1900	2000	2100	2200	2300	2400	100	200	300	400	500	600	700	800
1000	1100	1200	1300	1400	1500	1600	1700	1800	1900	2000	2100	2200	2300	2400	100	200	300	400	500	600	700	800	900
1100	1200	1300	1400	1500	1600	1700	1800	1900	2000	2100	2200	2300	2400	100	200	300	400	500	600	700	800	900	1000
1200	1300	1400	1500	1600	1700	1800	1900	2000	2100	2200	2300	2400	100	200	300	400	500	600	700	800	900	1000	1100
1300	1400	1500	1600	1700	1800	1900	2000	2100	2200	2300	2400	100	200	300	400	500	600	700	800	900	1000	1100	1200
1400	1500	1600	1700	1800	1900	2000	2100	2200	2300	2400	100	200	300	400	500	600	700	800	900	1000	1100	1200	1300
1500	1600	1700	1800	1900	2000	2100	2200	2300	2400	100	200	300	400	500	600	700	800	900	1000	1100	1200	1300	1400
1600	1700	1800	1900	2000	2100	2200	2300	2400	100	200	300	400	500	600	700	800	900	1000	1100	1200	1300	1400	1500
1700	1800	1900	2000	2100	2200	2300	2400	100	200	300	400	500	600	700	800	900	1000	1100	1200	1300	1400	1500	1600
1800	1900	2000	2100	2200	2300	2400	100	200	300	400	500	600	700	800	900	1000	1100	1200	1300	1400	1500	1600	1700
1900	2000	2100	2200	2300	2400	100	200	300	400	500	600	700	800	900	1000	1100	1200	1300	1400	1500	1600	1700	1800
2000	2100	2200	2300	2400	100	200	300	400	500	600	700	800	900	1000	1100	1200	1300	1400	1500	1600	1700	1800	1900
2100	2200	2300	2400	100	200	300	400	500	600	700	800	900	1000	1100	1200	1300	1400	1500	1600	1700	1800	1900	2000
2200	2300	2400	100	200	300	400	500	600	700	800	900	1000	1100	1200	1300	1400	1500	1600	1700	1800	1900	2000	2100
2300	2400	100	200	300	400	500	600	700	800	900	1000	1100	1200	1300	1400	1500	1600	1700	1800	1900	2000	2100	2200
2400	100	200	300	400	500	600	700	800	900	1000	1100	1200	1300	1400	1500	1600	1700	1800	1900	2000	2100	2200	2300

International Date Line — Today / Tomorrow

Figure 1. International Time Zone chart—how to tell what time it is anywhere else in the world.

your own time zone and read to the right or left until you reach the zone or place in which you are interested.

This chart has its limitations: (1) No consideration is given to Daylight Saving Time since not all countries adopt Daylight Saving Time and even those that do adopt it may not observe a uniform period of change; and (2) there is not always a full hour's difference between cities in different zones. To find the correct Standard Time for any place not given on the chart, look up the ± number in any International Time Zone chart and find the appropriate column; for a place listed as having a half-hour difference included (e.g., +3½) use the half hour between columns for +3 and +4.

Times given to the left of the zig-zag line are the same day (today) and those on the right are for the next day (tomorrow); or, conversely, if your time at the moment is on the right of the zig-zag line, this is today and the times on the left are for the day before, or yesterday. This means you need not remember that you add one day when you cross the International Date Line going west and you subtract one day when you cross it going east. For example, if you are traveling between Honolulu and Tokyo, find your time of departure and the corresponding time at your destination, add the estimated travel time, and you will know from the chart what time you will arrive and on what day. If you leave Honolulu at 10:00 a.m. on Monday, you arrive in Tokyo at 5:00 a.m. on Tuesday plus travel time; if you leave Tokyo at 5:00 a.m. on Tuesday, you arrive in Honolulu at 10:00 a.m. on Monday, plus travel time.

You will readily determine that there is no way you can telephone many of the major cities of the world when you are both open for business. In this case, if a telephone conversation between two executives is essential, prior arrangements should be made by letter or cable. For example, your executive can call from New York at 10:00 p.m. and reach Tokyo at 10:00 a.m. tomorrow—this will be during Tokyo business hours if you determine that "tomorrow" does not fall on a weekend.

The chart assumes you are familiar with the use of the 2400-hour method of determining time, rather than our own system of using a.m. and p.m. Any time up to 1200 hours is a.m., 1200 hours means noon; any time after 1200 hours is p.m. (to get the p.m. time, simply subtract 1200 hours) and 2400 is midnight.

Proper use of the telephone

The telephone has contributed greatly to the expansion and acceleration of business and industry, not only in this country, but throughout the world. There are ways to use and misuse the office telephone, however, and we will look at both.

We have reviewed the beginning and ending of telephone conversations, and now we will look at what goes on in between. You have probably made a call for your executive; "Mr. Smith wishes to speak with Mr. McDonald." The secretary says "Yes, he is here. Will you put Mr. Smith on the line, please." Tell Mr. Smith "Mr. McDonald's secretary is on the line—Mr. McDonald is available to speak with you now." This will alert your boss to expect the secretary on the line rather than McDonald, so that he will pick up the phone and say "Smith speaking" rather than "Hello, Ralph?"

Should a call come in for Mr. Smith, tell him "Mr. McDonald is calling. His secretary is on the line." Here again, you are telling him what to expect when he picks up the phone. Never argue with another secretary about whose boss is to be put on the line first—few executives object to a delay of only a few seconds. If a secretary asks that you put your boss on the line first, she may have the type of executive who has directed her to do so. The end result desired is to get Smith and McDonald together on the telephone without undue delay.

Suppose the incoming call is for you or is something you would normally handle, or suppose you have initiated the call and expect to take care of the matter. Be as brief as possible, but be sure you have given or obtained all the information necessary before concluding the call. Have your notes or correspondence before you while you are conversing so that it will not be necessary for either of you to call back with an "I forgot to ask you a few minutes ago . . ."

About some people it has been said that they have "no terminal facilities." Be sure this does not apply to you. A general rule of etiquette is that the calling party terminates the conversation. If you are the caller, then once you have completed your purpose, terminate the call with an appropriate "thank you." If the other person is the one who initiated the call and can't seem to wind it up, help him out by saying "It was a pleasure to look it up for you—call us anytime." If the other person is difficult to shake, you can always plead pressure of business. "I'm sorry, but I'll have to hang up—I have an urgent letter to get in the next mail."

Some secretaries still have failed to get the message about personal calls in the office. Any reasonable executive will realize that certain personal calls need to be made by his secretary during office hours. A five-minute call to make an appointment with a doctor or dentist, for example, would hardly be subject to criticism. A good secretary will use discretion in using the office telephone for personal calls and will always hold them to a minimum.

How to improve your telephone voice

Have you ever talked to yourself on the telephone? If so, how do you sound? If you have not, talk into a telephone tape recorder using comments and conversations similar to those you use every day and see for yourself.

1. Do you sound friendly, cheerful and helpful? Gestures and facial expressions carry favorably or unfavorably even over the telephone. The telephone company emphasizes the "voice with a smile." It's difficult to be, or to sound, grouchy when you're smiling, and difficult to be, or to sound, pleasant, when you're scowling. The person on the other end of the line has only the sound of your voice and your words to interpret

your message. Remember, too, that although the person on the telephone can't see your facial expressions, other people can. Visitors in the office, your executive, even people passing in the hall may be watching you—look your best!

2. Do you sound alert, interested, and capable? You should be brisk without being abrupt, interested with your comments and questions, and capable by supplying the appropriate information or referring the other person to the proper source.

3. Do you get the message across that the other person has your undivided attention? No matter how wild things are at the office, concentrate on the matter at hand. Be brief and to the point, but for the duration of the call, give your complete and personal attention.

4. Do you use proper grammar? And how is your diction? A secretary should know her grammar, so this should be no problem. But what about diction? There is nothing grammatically wrong with asking "What is your number?" But be sure you don't pronounce it "Whachernumber?" Be careful to speak clearly and distinctly over the telephone, and don't talk too fast; you should have to give your message only once. Speak directly into the mouthpiece, and don't garble your words.

5. Do you sigh, heave, and sound like a tired bovine who can't wait for the five o'clock whistle? *Example:* "I called about (sigh) the problem of a purchase requisition (heave) that I can't seem to locate. (Deep breath, another sigh.) It's for a printing calculator (heave) . . ." by this time, the other party is also yawning.

6. Do you sound as if you're in pain when you talk? *Example:* "I called (pause, voice obviously forced over pain in stomach, arthritic back, acute corns, etc.) to arrange an appointment (groan). . . ."

7. Do you speak naturally, without affectation? Your telephone voice should be the same as your voice in face-to-face conversation.

8. Do you "bark" into the telephone? *Example:* You dial a number and you know from experience to hold the receiver well away from your ear, because the telephone is answered with a blast: "MR. AYRES' OFFICE!"

9. Do you say "Do you have a minute" and then talk 30? Do you repeat yourself? Don't be the kind of person about whom it can be said "I would call her, but that would kill an hour. I'll send her a note."

Chapter 2

PROCESSING OFFICE
MAIL EFFICIENTLY

NO MATTER WHERE YOU WORK, as a secretary you know that over the past several years the paper going into and out of an office continues to increase at an accelerating rate. An obvious problem to the secretary is how to cope with this mountain of paper that crosses her desk—the in-plant or interoffice mail, outside correspondence, bulk mail and advertising, magazines, articles and publications, reports and manuscripts, and furthermore the volume of forms, material addressed to "general distribution" or the like, copies of office policies and procedures, either new or revised, and information copies of correspondence.

The estimate of the U.S. Postal Service that many billion pieces of mail are transported within the United States each year is impressive. A representative of the U.S. Postal Service made this point vividly some time ago when he said that if all the mail posted in this country in one year were loaded on freight cars, the train required to carry it would have its engine in California and its caboose in New York.

Proper handling of office paper is, therefore, a primary responsibility of the secretary. In this chapter we will consider ways to cope with this particular office problem.

"Dating" in the office

A secretary never fails to "date" anything that comes across her desk, whether it originates outside her office or within her office. A piece of paper received (even bulk mail which may ultimately end up in the waste basket) should be stamped with at least the date, possibly the hour and moment (time stamp) when she first receives it. A piece of paper originating in her office should certainly bear the date (month, day, and year) and, if necessary, the actual time of dispatch.

Examples of frustration because of lack of information with regard to date might include the following: (1) A sales report for the quarter July, August, and September—but guess what year? (2) A summary comparison of employment for the past two fiscal years, plus anticipated employment during the next fiscal year, with no fiscal year identified. (3) A letter dated January 10, 1978, which is "in response to your letter of December 3, 1978." Which year is in error? Great care should be taken that any date appearing on any piece of paper is correct.

A note reading "confirming our conversation of today" should bear the date of the conversation, regardless of the date the note is typed. Even better is to type the note to agree with the facts: "March 16, 1978: Confirming our conversation of March 15, ... "

Notations on office correspondence should always be dated. "To Purchasing Department 7/13/77 for action." "To J. A. Smith 6/23/77: Please advise." This serves notice to the person to whom the paper is referred that even though the original letter was dated two months ago, action was requested much later—and you have a note to remind you that a letter dated April 23 reached you on June 15 (as indicated by the "received" stamp and your initials) and was handled promptly by your office.

A copy of material sent from your office should bear the date it was forwarded or copied and sent. A report for the fiscal year ending December 31, 1977, received in your office and so identified by a date stamp showing that the finished copy was received on January 31, 1978, should bear a notation by date when another copy was furnished to another office or installation. "Copy 2/3/78 for H. J. Beatty."

Identification of sender and receiver

Equally important is the identification as to who sent or received a piece of mail. How interesting to receive a statistical report which is neither dated nor identified as to who prepared it! An executive should not be required to play guessing games, which he may sometimes have to do if he receives a draft in an envelope with no return address, no identifying initials either as to dictator, typist, or date prepared. Of no help on a document of this type is a cryptic typed note, also unsigned, undated, and unidentified with initials, which reads "let me have your comments by Tuesday."

Often a legal question will arise as to when a piece of mail was received and by whom. Sometimes a possible legal implication can be inferred by a competent secretary, but the best way to avoid the need for such interpretation is to have as much proof as possible of time of receipt on every piece of mail. A good secretary will develop the habit of routinely documenting the date (and perhaps time as well) and using at least her initials on each piece of incoming mail to indicate when it was received in her office.

How to process incoming mail in record time

Secretaries have been known to announce with martrydom "I haven't had time to open the morning mail!" In some offices, where the morning mail is no more important than the afternoon mail (meaning that nothing of significance ever comes into the office), her executive is probably not concerned. This is not true in an effective office at any level of management. The office mail, regardless of when it arrives, should receive immediate attention, second only to the telephone which refuses to be ignored. Not all of the mail may require immediate or priority attention, but it should at least be opened so that any important correspondence can be brought to your executive's attention immediately.

We assume, of course, that a secretary can separate the important from the unimportant mail. A report of the company picnic held two weeks ago, for example, can be read within the next day or so with presumably no adverse effects on the company profit margin. An airmail letter from a client regarding a $50,000 order is another matter.

Remembering that a capable secretary relieves her executive of as much detail as possible, you are able to decide, on first reading the incoming mail, what your executive will want to handle personally, what should be forwarded to another member of the organization, what you can take care of yourself, and what requires no action.

A secretary is usually expected to open the mail that comes into the office—after a discussion of the matter with her executive. If he so directs, she opens *all* the mail, even that marked "personal and confidential." An exception is that marked "To be opened by addressee only." In this case, as well as with personal and/or confidential mail, if he prefers to open it himself, she should stamp and initial the date received on the envelope, open a slot about an inch in length at one corner to facilitate his completing the opening, and include it with the other opened and suitably annotated mail.

Some of the incoming mail should be directed to the executive for his personal attention: Examples include matters concerning important and/or technical business or a personal letter.

For bulk mail, advertisements, unsolicitated catalogs and magazines, routine announcements of meetings and the like, have an understanding with him as to what you will discard after his review unless he directs otherwise.

You can help your fellow secretaries increase their

speed in opening the incoming mail if you seal your first-class mail properly. Sealing the envelope serves two purposes: (1) It helps to make sure that the material inside the envelope does not fall out and get lost, and (2) it protects the contents from preview by other people before it reaches its destination. Both purposes can be served by sealing the envelope in the center only; in fact, some envelopes are made with the glue provided only to within an inch of either end of the envelope or with unglued spaces between the glue. This makes it easy to insert a letter opener and open the envelop with one quick flip.

Whatever you do, whether the mail is marked personal, addressee only, or any other special handling, do *not* seal it with tape so that a letter opener cannot be inserted at some point in the envelope closure. The envelope must be opened by some means if the contents are to be removed, and, if it must be cut with scissors, some of the contents may also be cut.

Advantages of a mail register*

Whether or not you use a mail register depends upon your own office. Examples of mail registers can be found in secretarial handbooks, but you may want to develop your own. Some advantages of using a register are these:

1. Correspondence can be located by date, by author, or by subject.
2. It's easy for another secretary to locate correspondence in your absence, or for your executive to do so himself, if necessary.
3. You have a record of items passed to someone else with no copy retained in your office.
4. It serves as a quick "catch up" on what occurred while you were away from the office.

---

*Thanks to two CPS's for help on this section: Peggy Courtney, Baton Rouge, Louisiana, and Nelline Ross, Oak Ridge, Tennessee.

5. The action date serves as a tickler to remind you when to remind your executive, or another office, of the action required.

6. It reminds you when a letter prepared in another office for your executive's signature has not yet been dispatched.

7. It's much easier to flip through a mail register than to search through the number of documents it represents.

Since this is an internal working tool to keep track of correspondence, recording is usually done by hand—so long as the information is legible, there is no need to waste time in typing it.

Figure 2 is an example of registers used to record incoming and outgoing correspondence.

Handle each piece of mail as little as possible

Handle each piece of paper as little as possible. If you can, take care of the paper the moment you receive it—when it comes out of the envelope is the best time. Check for required action: personal attention of your executive; routing to another person; providing your own input; or discarding it once it has crossed the executive's desk—and do as much of what is required at that moment. Date-stamp each piece of mail with your initials beside the stamp and insert the file code as appropriate. Indicate action required by use of a route slip or a note. Draft, or prepare in final form, a response or acknowledgment of the paper before you send it in to your executive.

How to expedite outgoing mail after it leaves your office

Once your mail is in the out-box, be sure you have done all you can to expedite its delivery. Is your return address, including zip code, on every envelope? Is the address properly

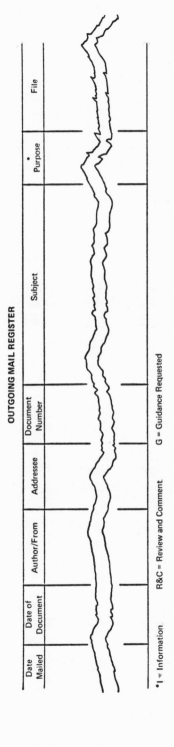

Figure 2. Sample mail registers—for outgoing and incoming mail.

OUTGOING MAIL REGISTER

Date Mailed	Date of Document	Author/From	Addressee	Document Number	Subject	Purpose *	File

*I = Information   R&C = Review and Comment   G = Guidance Requested

INCOMING MAIL REGISTER

Date Received	Date of Document	Author	Addressee	Subject/Doc. Ident. No.	Action/Date *	Routed To	Handled By	Filed

*R = Reply   F = Follow Up   IO = Information Only

typed, with zip code and proper notation if something other than first class is desired?

There is no reason for a secretary to be unaware of the proper way to address and mail correspondence, printed material, magazines or newspapers, or packages anywhere in the United States—or abroad. Any United States Post Office has a number of pamphlets which are yours upon request, at no charge, to assist you with your mailing problems. Much attention has been given in the past several years to the use of computers in expediting mail service, and of primary importance is the use of the zip code. A further computerized effort is the use of two-letter abbreviations for the names of states, to be used *only* with zip codes. The two-letter abbreviations used in the U.S. mail system are given in Figure 3.

In a computerized postal operation in metropolitan areas, a first-class piece of correspondence addressed to John Doe, Los Angeles, California, would likely be (1) returned to the sender if a return address is on the envelope, or (2) destroyed if no return address is given.

To assure efficient delivery in the United States of mail dispatched from your office, therefore, there are certain rules to follow:

(1) Be sure the address is as complete as possible, accurate, that your spelling is correct, and that you include the correct zip code.

(2) If the material is other than first class, be sure it is properly identified as to class, handling, etc. Classes of mail are as follows:

First class: Letters, post cards, handwritten or type-written communications or copies of such communications

Second class: Newspapers and periodicals

Third class: Printed matter up to 16 ounces; packages (parcel post) weighing between 1 and 40 pounds

State	Former Abbr.	Now	State	Former Abbr.	Now
Alabama	Ala.	AL	Montana	Mont.	MT*
Alaska	—	AK*	Nebraska	Neb.	NE
Arizona	Ariz.	AZ*	Nevada	Nev.	NV*
Arkansas	Ark.	AR	New Hampshire	N. H.	NH
California	Calif.	CA	New Jersey	N. J.	NJ
Colorado	Colo.	CO	New Mexico	N. M.	NM
Connecticut	Conn.	CT*	New York	N. Y.	NY
Delaware	Del.	DE	North Carolina	N. C.	NC
District of			North Dakota	N. D.	ND
Columbia	D. C.	DC	Ohio	—	OH
Florida	Fla.	FL	Oklahoma	Okla.	OK
Georgia	Ga.	GA	Oregon	Ore.	OR
Hawaii	—	HI*	Pennsylvania	Pa.	PA
Idaho	—	ID	Rhode Island	R. I.	RI
Illinois	Ill.	IL	South Carolina	S. C.	SC
Indiana	Ind.	IN	South Dakota	S. D.	SD
Iowa	—	IA*	Tennessee	Tenn.	TN*
Kansas	Kans.	KS*	Texas	Tex.	TX*
Kentucky	Ky.	KY	Utah	—	UT
Louisiana	La.	LA	Vermont	Vt.	VT
Maine	Me.	ME	Virginia	Va.	VA
Maryland	Md.	MD	Washington	Wash.	WA
Massachusetts	Mass.	MA	West Virginia	W. Va.	WV
Michigan	Mich.	MI	Wisconsin	Wis.	WI
Minnesota	Minn.	MN*	Wyoming	Wyo.	WY
Mississippi	Miss.	MS*			
Missouri	Mo.	MO	Puerto Rico	P. R.	PR

*Note that most of the two-letter abbreviations are the first letter of each word of a two-word state, the first two letters of the name of the state, or the former accepted abbreviation. Only the 12 exceptions need be learned.

Figure 3. Two-letter State abbreviations used by the U.S. Postal Service

Fourth class: Printed matter over 16 ounces and up to 40 pounds, no larger than 84 inches, length and girth combined; books and reports consisting of at least 24 pages and permanently bound, weight limit 70 pounds

With computerization, a certain format is required to permit the computers to operate at maximum efficiency. In general, the address is typed as has been customary for a number of years. Exceptions are these:

a. With the zip code, use the two-letter abbreviations for names of states.

b. If the material is anything but first class, be sure the notation appears in the *upper* part of the address; this includes notations of Special Delivery, Air Mail, Special Handling, etc. Such notations should be *not lower* than the line above the city, state, and zip code.

c. If an attention line is used on the envelope, it, too, should not be lower than the line above the city, state, and zip code. The U.S. Postal Service prefers that it be done this way:

MANY PRODUCTS, INC.
ATTN: MR. JOHN DOE, SALES MANAGER
ANYTOWN XX   12345

d. If a letter to be airmailed is sent in other than a distinctive, thin-paper airmail envelope, be sure to indicate airmail prominently. This is best achieved on a plain envelope by stamping or typing the word "airmail" two spaces above the address, and perhaps (for insurance) left of the address, not lower than the line above the city, state, and zip code.

e. Other special directions to the U.S. Postal Service should be indicated, preferably in a conspicuous spot on the envelope such as under the stamps (or postal meter stamp).

(3) If you do not understand the difference between the postal services available, check with your local post office. Among other things, you will learn that "Special Delivery" is of no help when the address is to a post office box or a rural route; if a street address is given, the post office will "special deliver" the mail to the addressee after business hours, on a weekend, or on a holiday. Special delivery to a post office box has been accomplished when the mail has been placed in the appropriate box. "Special Handling" does not guarantee special care of your mail; it merely assures you that there will be no delay between transfer points. For example, if mail from the point of origin to point of destination requires transfer from one train or plane to another railroad or airline, the transfer will be handled expeditiously rather than routinely.

Reading the office mail*

An efficient secretary not only opens the office mail, she reads it, or at least scans it for content. She is not expected to read and try to comprehend lengthy technical reports or the like, but she should read enough of whatever crosses her desk so that she will be able to discharge her responsibilities properly.

You must read enough of an incoming piece of mail to determine where and if it should be filed. Failure to do so may result in misfiling, where retrieval can be accomplished only through accident.

You must read enough of an incoming letter to determine whether a reply is required, and if so, when. The letter may need an immediate acknowledgment with a follow-up for a detailed reply by a certain date. For example, an incoming letter may ask if your company is interested in submitting a bid for a

---

*This section is included with thanks to Peggy Courtney, C.P.S., Baton Rouge, Louisiana, for the outline.

certain job within the next 30 days. If your company *is* interested, the letter should be acknowledged immediately and the preparation of the bid scheduled to meet the stated deadline. While the major responsibility for the matter lies with your executive, you should be aware of the work flow in your office and be prepared to remind your executive of the approaching deadline. Don't let a letter "fall between the desks" in your office.

When you read the incoming mail, note carefully not only the company name on the letterhead, but also the name and title of the writer. Be knowledgeable about the names of clients and customers, or potential ones, so that you never make the mistake of brushing off an unexpected caller who should be given the red-carpet treatment. A good secretary knows, or makes it her business to find out, the names of people and companies who are important to her executive.

Incoming mail should be read to determine what, if any, background material should be obtained from your files or from another office before the correspondence is given to your executive. Time is saved for both you and your executive if the background information is obtained as soon as possible after you realize it is needed. Twice the time is required if your executive must ask you for the needed material, wait for you to get it, and then re-review the correspondence.

You should read enough of the incoming mail to determine who in your organization should receive a copy. If John Doe should have a copy immediately of a particular incoming letter or report, check to see if his name is on the distribution list. If not, see that he gets a copy as immediately as possible. Avoid giving your office the reputation of being a bottleneck.

Read the incoming mail for possible upcoming appointments. "I'll be in town on the 23rd and would like to see you at 11:00 a.m. if that's convenient." Make a note on your appointment schedule as soon as you have read the letter; you can always cross it off if the time suggested is *not* convenient, but having the note on your calendar may prevent scheduling a conflicting appointment.

"Enclosed are the tentative plans for the new shopping center at East Gate." You don't have to examine the plans (unless that is your responsibility), but you should read the transmittal letter carefully enough to recall, if asked, that you have received the letter and that the plans were enclosed. (If they were not, make a suitable note on the letter.)

In summary, your responsibility as an efficient secretary is not only to open the mail, but to know what's in it.

Things to consider if your mail is going overseas

In today's ever-expanding business world, more and more companies are corresponding and doing business with people and organizations in foreign countries. While postal regulations in this country and abroad are similar in many respects, there are significant differences of which a good secretary should be aware. We will disucss a few of them in this section.

In addressing an envelope to be delivered in a foreign country, follow the same format used *in the foreign country*. The name of the country is always on the bottom line, usually in caps and sometimes underscored for the benefit of the U.S. Postal Service. The numbering system used in some other countries, similar to our zip code, is important in expediting delivery of U.S. mail once it has reached the foreign country. However, in some cases the equivalent zip number will follow the name of the country and in other cases will precede it. Whereas in the United States we normally follow the name of the addressee with the appropriate number and street, then the city and state, some countries follow the name of the addressee with the city and then the street and number. If you copy the foreign address exactly as it is given, you will assist the foreign postal service in delivering your mail expeditiously.

There is no need to translate a foreign address into English. The name of the country is always in English, but the rest of the address should be typed the way it is given; and if it is given in another language, type it that way, writing in the diacritical marks if you don't have the appropriate keys on your typewriter.

U.S. postage is good only in the United States except

for mail sent out of a foreign country by a U.S. government agency, such as the military service. Therefore, do not send a self-addressed envelope overseas with a U.S. stamp on it; to be handled by a foreign postal service, the mail going *out* of that country must carry an indication that postage has been paid to the appropriate foreign government.

Airmail letters will usually be delivered abroad in about five days. "Surface mail" (anything other than airmail) may require several weeks for delivery. About the same time requirement applies for airmail and surface mail coming to the U.S. from abroad, and "abroad" includes Canada and Mexico. All first-class mail going abroad, therefore, should be sent airmail. Surface mail may be used for any material, especially that of any bulk such as heavy reports, not required by the recipient for at least six weeks. The determining factor in how material is sent abroad is not the weight or the cost, but the delivery time desired.

Not all the postal services provided in the United States are available in all foreign countries. For example, mail to some countries can be insured or registered, but to others it cannot. Packages with addresses to certain foreign countries may or may not be delivered relatively intact to the addressee. Your U.S. Post Office will be able to help you if you have any question about the services provided by any foreign country. Be especially sure to check the best way to dispatch your foreign mail, if you aren't certain, before you mail anything of value.

Chapter 3

PRACTICAL FILING AND
RETRIEVAL METHODS

W HAT'S THE FIRST THING A SECRETARY DOES when she comes to work in the morning? Gets a cup of coffee, of course. What's the last thing she does, and usually only when everything else is caught up? She files the office papers—or at least, she puts them out of sight.

But there is more to filing than office housekeeping. Filing is a most important part of office routine and can be both interesting and a challenge.

You know the different methods of filing: Alphabetic, geographic, numerical, or a combination—including the Dewey decimal. Your present system may be just as good as any other, provided you can find what you have filed. And a must is to *file* by the system you will use to *retrieve*. In other words, if you file by "f" for "fridge" know what you're doing and don't try to retrieve the information by looking under "r" for refrigerator.

If there is a standard system of filing used throughout your organization, you may be able to modify the standard system to serve your own specific needs more effectively.

How to do 50 percent of your filing
without leaving your chair

Your executive may prefer to make the decision as to whether material is to be filed, and if so, where. However, if the responsibility is left to you, here are some suggestions.

To do half your filing without leaving your chair, note on the paper the first time it crosses your desk where it is to be filed. The note can be a number or a word or two. If you aren't certain where the paper properly belongs, put a question mark in pencil—this will remind you to check further, or ask your executive, before you make a decision. For example, the note may be "Sales—Colorado"; it may be 600.06; or it may be #1 (designating the file on the extreme left or right) with a subnotation "a", "b", "c", etc., denoting the drawer. A good place for the note is the upper right-hand corner of the page.

Underscore key words in the correspondence with a red pencil or a "highlighter" pen for ready reference when you are actually placing the paper in the folder. Another helpful hint is to decide the first time you see it whether the paper is to be filed in an appropriate folder or discarded. If the latter, a simple designation such as "x" will indicate that you have read the paper once, made your decision, and therefore you know what to do with it when it comes back from your executive.

Some pieces of paper are for information only, and a brief notation on a register, card, or other simplified record will permit immediate destruction of the paper. If the major responsibility for filing papers lies with another office and you are interested only in the information contained in the papers, there is no need to keep duplicate copies. A card system, a register, or whatever seems appropriate should be adequate for your own office. Make the appropriate notation on your card file or register for reference, and send your copy (original or duplicate) to the appropriate office for file.

A file index will be helpful to both you and your executive. List on letter-size paper the labels of your file drawers and the sections in each drawer, perhaps even down to each folder; keep a copy at your desk and give one to your executive. This will help you code your papers for filing without leaving your chair and will also be useful in a number of other ways. For example, you will be able to determine readily by scanning the index if you have an appropriate folder for a particular piece of information; if you have a number of filing cabinets, you can determine at a glance where you should look for information related to incoming correspondence or for something which has been requested; if you are asked to summarize a certain activity or program for which your office is responsible, the index can be used as a checklist to be sure you haven't overlooked something which should be included. A file index is also very helpful to anyone who is substituting for you when you are away from the office. A brief outline of a hypothetical file index is illustrated in Figure 4-a on page 48.

Shortcuts to filing and finding
business papers

Filing a piece of paper in an overstuffed miscellaneous folder takes little time in the beginning, but may require minutes of retrieval time. As soon as several papers accumulate on a single subject or project, your time is well spent to simply label an additional folder so that, when called for, all information available on the matter can be produced in a matter of seconds.

The executive who dictates a memorandum or a letter on each separate subject makes filing a delight for his secretary; however, some executives will frequently dictate material in one piece of correspondence that covers two, three, or more subjects. To be sure that the necessary information is available in each pertinent file, therefore, you must either reproduce a copy for each file or "cross-index." Decide for yourself whether it is simpler to make additional copies or to set up a cross index, which can be done in a number of ways. One way is to insert a letter-size piece of paper, in chronological order in each file, with a notation (cross reference) of the date, subject, to and

WHICH FILING SYSTEM DO YOU USE?

EFFECTIVE   HAPHAZARD

Figure 4-b. An effective filing system illustrated here is made possible with the use of Oxford Pendaflex folders. Check with your office supply company for additional information, or write to Oxford Pendaflex Corporation, 74 Clinton Road, Garden City, NY 11530.

SAMPLE FILE INDEX

Budget, Accounting, and Finance

Bank Statements
Budget Estimates
Financial Statements
Insurance
Payrolls
Taxes

Office Files

Address Lists
Daily File
Postal Information
Records Maintenance
Transportation Services

Organization and Management

Organization Charts
Directives
Office Methods and Practices

Personnel

Employment
Salaries and Wages
Labor Relations
Benefit Plans
Health and Safety

Figure 4-a.
Sample File Index

from, etc., and the file where the correspondence may be found. Another way is to develop your own form to staple to the front of the folder with a place for date, subject, to, from, file, etc., to indicate that if the material wanted is not included in this particular file, it might appear in another one or two.

Since filing is usually on the bottom of the list with respect to a secretary's performance of office duties, it is sometimes necessary to emphasize the importance of filing properly so that any piece of paper desired can be retrieved instantly. Your executive is in his office on long-distance, perhaps to Europe, and he suddenly demands, and expects immediately, a piece of paper concerning the subject of his conversation. "Ms. X, let me have that paper on the contract for bauxite with the ABC company—we received it sometime last month." If you can produce the paper within a matter of seconds, you need not worry when your time for a merit increase comes up.

"Lost" papers which seemingly cannot be found anywhere in the office are quite often caused by the paper clip. Manifold (or onionskin) sheets are especially prone to "take up" with a nearby paper clip which is holding together material completely unrelated to the hitch-hiker. Avoid fastening papers with paper clips when they are to be filed. If you prefer not to fasten papers permanently in the appropriate folder, use staples to keep related materials together for ready reference.

Remember that the most important part of filing is retrieving. Make your system the "effective" rather than the "haphazard" (see Figure 4-b). Time is well spent in setting up a new folder or a new section in your filing system, replacing battered folders or labels, retiring or destroying records which are no longer needed in your office, or doing anything else necessary to make your retrieval system more efficient.

The secretary is responsible for producing from the files the desired piece of paper, the necessary information to compile a report, the back-up to rebut a lawsuit, or any amount and kind of information which is supposed to be in her office. In general, you should keep copies of any correspondence generated by your executive. You should file any information pertinent to the responsibilities of your office, any directives concerning company policy or procedures, and any information which is not likely to be available in any other office in the organization.

Color can make your filing system more efficient. File folders, tabs, separators, etc., come in every color. Assume that you are secretary to the Vice-President of Sales: Yellow represents the midwest, pink is the northeast, blue is southeast, and green is southwest. Use these colors for the separators and white labels in each area to denote monthly reports, volume, product movement, expense accounts, etc. If, within each group, there are subfiles which need to be set up, use orange with yellow, cerise with pink, navy with blue, and pistachio with green—or any other colors you wish. You will find your office supply companies most helpful in assisting with your selections.

Save filing time—how to decide what goes into the wastebasket

Decide as soon as a piece of paper crosses your desk whether it is to be filed or destroyed, and if it is to be destroyed, when. An example is a note of a routine meeting—once your executive has attended the meeting, the notice of why, when, and where can be destroyed. An exception, of course, is an important meeting where it might be necessary to prove the date and time of the receipt of the notice. Another possibility for destruction includes a lot of bulk mail advertising. Ask your executive what you should do with such unsolicited advertising, and suggest that, unless he indicates to the contrary, it be discarded once he has reviewed it.

Discuss your filing system with your executive and explain that a notation on the paper indicates that it is to be filed and retrieved sometime in the future—unless the note is an "x." If he does not want the material destroyed, he should cross out the "x" and note what is to be done with it ("file," "forward to," etc.).

How and when to dispose of office files

Some papers need to be kept for a time and then destroyed. Examples are: (1) Lists of materials available at a special price through a certain date—once the date has passed, there is usually no further need for the list; (2) information given for the end of a quarter which becomes obsolete when the next quarter's information is available; (3) material which will be needed for reference only for a certain period, such as a month, a quarter, or a year; once it is superseded, it can be destroyed. A systematic method for "retiring" such information should be developed.

Material to be "retired" may be handled in a number of ways. If a folder is to contain information no more than "x" days/weeks/months, it may be labeled that way. For example, a folder containing information that will be useless after it is three months old should be labeled "3 Mo.", and when April's information is filed, December's should be disposed of. Another way to "retire" files is to send them to storage (a central records station, a warehouse, etc.). These are records which are not presently needed in your office, and for which no immediate need in the future is foreseen; but there is a possibility that they may be required under the "statute of limitations" sometime in the future, say three to five years hence. These records can be stored in cartons or transfiles which are clearly marked "Destroy in 1980 if not called for before then."

How to remember everything
without even thinking

Write it down! It makes no difference where or how, but write it down where you will find it when it's time to do something about it. This is sometimes called a "tickler" file. And a tickler file can be anything—from a note on the calendar to a pending file, to a daily, weekly, monthly, or yearly reminder, to a scrap of paper stuck in the corner of your desk blotter.

Maybe there are certain things you need to do every Monday, or any other day in the week. For example, if you are responsible for the weekly payroll, checks must be made out on the same day each week; keep a note of that on your daily tickler file. If the monthly sales report is due on the tenth of the month, note this on your tickler file by date. Some reports or data are due quarterly, annually, or semiannually by a certain date—note this on your yearly reminder. Note only what is necessary: Monday is blank if there is nothing specifically due on Monday, but Tuesday may be crowded with certain things to check, to do, or to bring to the attention of your executive.

Leave your office today, confident that, should anything keep you away from the office tomorrow, someone else could take over and get the job done respectably for the company simply by referring to your records.

Not all the days of the month will have something to check, but routinize your work as much as possible and check every folder; or card, or index on each day of the month to see if there is something you should be checking or doing on that particular day. And don't forget to check on Friday for what may fall due on a date that happens to be on a weekend this month.

If a report requires two or three days' preparation time, counting normal office interruptions, "tickle" yourself two or three days before the report is due. Do not martyr yourself by spending your lunch period or overtime getting a job done that you could have completed routinely if you had only started sooner.

Executives ask all kinds of questions, and you should be prepared to answer them if you are expected to have the information. "Is today Rotary?" "Are we having a Board meeting this afternoon?" "When is the next Council meeting?" "Is my wife's birthday this month?" Check your tickler file for the proper reply!

There are any number of prepared "tickler's" on the market, but you can make your own. A simple sheet of paper for day, week, or month, may suffice. Quarterly reports are indicated only four times a year, and annual reports only once. If you are on a calendar-year basis, semiannual reports are prepared as of June 30 and December 31 (due dates vary) of each year, but if they are prepared on the basis of your company's fiscal year, "as of" dates may be different.

A miscellaneous "tickler" file may also be kept. This is simply a group of papers or information held in a pending file until action has been taken by another office—your only responsibility is to be sure that "please handle" or "prepare reply for my signature" or something similar is taken care of before the due date. This is a file where no particular date is marked for checking—but normally not for more than a few days or weeks. If the action date is months or a year or more in the future, a better tickler is on the calendar or the annual agenda.

An agenda is prepared for a meeting and contains items to be discussed and the order of business. An agenda serves a very useful purpose: it reminds the presiding officer of matters to be discussed and the order in which they are to be brought up. An annual agenda in the office serves an equally useful purpose: it reminds your executive of matters to be considered over a period of time, and the order in which they should be considered. For example, it alerts him to the need for consideration of summer employees before June 1 when most summer appointments begin; it reminds him that the heating system must be checked prior to the beginning of the winter season, or that the air-conditioning must be checked before the onset of summer; it reminds him that the members of the Board of Directors must be notified at least one month in advance of the annual meeting.

A tickler system can be a card file by day, week, month or year; it may be by file folder with the same divisions; it may be a single sheet of paper with the same divisions; it may be notes on your desk calendar. The important point of remembering everything without even thinking is to *write it down*, and be sure the item is brought to your attention, or to your executive's, in ample time to avoid a crisis because you forgot to remember.

Selecting an appropriate time to file

An ideal system of filing is to spend one part of each day, without fail, in filing papers. Depending upon your own particular office routine, the best time may be the first thing in the morning, or the last thing in the afternoon. On the other hand, the best time may be just before or after lunch or a coffee break. Piled-up filing always seems an interminable chore to tackle—avoid it; you can place a lot of paper properly in the files in 10 or 15 minutes.

Although the ideal situation is to file daily, so that all papers are in the proper folder and each folder is up to the minute, this is not always possible. To save time in trying to locate a paper which has crossed your desk within the past day or so, but which has not yet been inserted in the proper folder, place a tray on top of each filing cabinet and "first-sort" your papers by cabinet. If you have only one cabinet, the tray can be a tiered one (one tier for each drawer in the cabinet) and the pre-sort can be by drawer. However, for two or more cabinets, a single tray on top of each cabinet containing pre-sorted material will reduce searching time if you need a paper that has not yet been filed. In other words, to look for a paper which will ultimately be filed in cabinet "1", look in the tray on top of cabinet "1"; you won't have to look through all the papers which are yet to be filed in another cabinet.

If you can't place each paper in its proper folder before the end of the day, at least try to pre-sort, into a tray atop each cabinet, every day.

The many uses of the chron file

"Where is the letter I wrote to what's-his-name sometime last month about 3' steel lathes?" or something similarly vague is not an unusual request from executive to secretary. How do you look that up in the file? The chron file may help you. By keeping an extra copy of all outgoing correspondence, which is filed by date, you may need to look through a hundred pieces of paper as opposed to a hundred file folders to come up with the information required.

Suppose you want a new typewriter—on the basis of use. A healthy chron file showing that you have produced "x" inches of paper in the past number of months or years you have used your present typewriter will be some indication of the amount of typing you have produced and the amount of mileage on your typewriter.

Every copy of material produced, whether by carbon, copy machine, or printing process costs the company money. By making a copy do double duty, you will save the company money. The chron file copy need not be filed daily if it can serve another use prior to being filed. Keep it in a suspense file for checking purposes, putting the office copy in the regular file so that complete information on any particular subject is available by simply pulling the folder.

The chron file is an excellent reference for similar letters or paragraphs which may be used as a pattern to prepare, in draft or final form, a letter for your executive's signature. A careful reading of the chron file will also help a "new girl in the office" (you or someone else) to determine the writing style of the executive, to understand the type of correspondence peculiar to the office, and to get a better idea of the scope of the work with which the secretary will be involved.

Chapter 4

INCREASING TYPING
PRODUCTIVITY—WITH TIPS
FOR SPECIAL REPORTS

AS A SECRETARY, you have passed the test for required speed and accuracy in typing—these "requirements" vary, but a normal minimum requirement is 50 words a minute net. However, 50 words a minute net with two mistakes is better than 50 words a minute net with 10 mistakes. Why? Because time is required to correct an error. Two errors on a single page may be neatly corrected, but with ten errors, it may be necessary to retype the page to produce an acceptable piece of work. Whatever method you use to correct an error, concentrating on accuracy in typing, rather than speed, will increase your net words a minute.

Six ways to increase your typing speed and productivity

When taking a typing test, you know certain tricks will help you achieve maximum speed. You return the carriage the moment the bell rings, rather than begin another word and worry about dividing it, because you must stop and think about the word division as well has hit an extra stroke (the hyphen). Your test is normally a standard, straightforward piece of material with no foreign or technical words, symbols, or strings of numbers such as would appear in a financial statement. In other words, you are tested on your ability to type "straight" typing.

As a general rule, your speed on a typing test has no bearing on the speed with which you will be able to produce material on the job in which you are placed. Suppose you type 50 words a minute with two mistakes on a typing test—can you type a purchase requisition (form) at the rate of 50 words a minute? Not very likely. You may type 50 words a minute when you have an opportunity, but there is lost time when you have to use tab stops or fit your typing into the various sections or blocks, align your machine vertically or horizontally, and type such information as 3 @ 0.003¢ ea., nuts and bolts with tungsten lining, 3¼ x 5½ wt., 50,000/lb.

Assuming that you begin with a typing speed of 50 words a minute net with no more than two mistakes, which is only fair typing, how can you increase your typing speed and productivity? (Note that typing speed is one thing, typing productivity is another.) First we will begin with typing speed; that is, increasing your speed from 50 words a minute net with no more than two errors. There are many ways to increase your speed, but the following suggestions are almost guaranteed to increase your speed on what we will call "straight" typing:

1. KNOW YOUR KEYBOARD

If you are a typist at all, you know your letters, but what about the rest of the keyboard? The letter-keyboard is standard on all typewriters, but the rest of the keyboard will vary with the make and model of the machine.

See Figure 5 for a suggested typing test to check your skill in typing other than the conventional "a" through "z" letters. If your speed is still 50 words a minute with no more than two errors, you are truly an accomplished typist. Your speed will

	No. Words
L'intervento dei sistemi di refrigerazione del nocciolo	11
e/o spurzzamento del pozze secco puo mettere in depressione	23
tale ambiente rispetto alla camera di soppressione.	33
La diversite du comportemente des terrains selon leur	43
constitution montre qu'il sera necessaire d'etudier d'autres	55
phenomenes thermiques, en particulier la convection, pour les	67
milieux a pourcentage eleve en matiere liquide ou liquefiable.	79
Vor zwei Jahrzehnten begannenwir uns, fur diese Wech-	90
selwirkung zu interessieren – zu dieser Zeit unter dem Gesicht-	102
spunkt ihrer Auswirkungen in industrielen Prozessen im	113
Zusemmenhang mit der Umwandlung von Xolekulen im Erdol.	124
A foldreform eredmenyekeppen 1945-ben a fold vegre azoke	135
lett, akik megmuvelik a magyar gazdasagi elet atalakitasaert	147
vivott kuzdelem azonban meg ezzel korantsem dolt el a haladas	159
eroinek javara.	162
379* 14298& 67892# 3¢8%$ "-6&3 684310& 864-%7 209 867	173
62*8 68#0 72095 36&83 389 410 69 823#'67 48657 888425 $(67&3	185
1863542390 1@'3$ 67129#5 862847 3"7 84&¢32 319 (0)37¢413 05	197
6728&3¢ 694 21 8940¢732 -83¢96"2 10456&*)#9 671 32 489762	209
7/13/75.38 368-497-62 10752$38 @218463&¢-) 387 41 98765& *2	221
342/8-421 7/63/48.75 $1,002,386 42110. ¢75 38 982489 32516	233
887-654-983,---491/67/982, 463?906¢%--, 654, ¢304985854, 89	245
7634,%209,368/743/687¢. ¢6&7*8(9)1, 2396734; 868"364', 10!	257

Check your typing speed on this material which includes nonletter characters and languages other than English. Numbers at the end of each line are the total number of words to the end of that line. To compute gross words a minute on a five-minute test, divide the total number of words by five. To arrive at the net words a minute, subtract two words for each error.

Figure 5. A typing test to check your speed on unfamiliar material.

very likely be much less than on "straight" typing, because the emphasis in learning to type is generally on the letters, and the other characters are something to be learned "also." The "hunt and peck" system can be used when numbers or symbols are required in the text. But any typing assignment calls for a date, financial assignments call for tabulation, numbers, dollar signs, sometimes the @ (for "at" so much each), etc.; and in mathematical typing, symbols such as + and = are stumbling blocks. You may not be able to type numbers and symbols as fast as you can type "Now is the time. . .," but you should be adept and accurate, using the touch system, with every nonletter key on your typewriter.

Some typewriters have interchangeable or special keys or "balls" so that you can type mathematical symbols, Greek letters, diacritical marks, etc. An efficient typist will be able to type at relatively the same speed on any typewriter once she has identified the nonletter keys, assuming that she is using the same general type of machine. A change from manual portable to standard electric will increase your speed, and a change from a standard electric to a manual portable will take some of the speed away. A change from standard electric to executive electric will likewise decrease your speed until you become accustomed to the different features.

2. USE THE SPECIAL FEATURES
ON YOUR TYPEWRITER

Also on your keyboard, but not a part of the characters which can be reproduced by the process of striking the keys, are a number of supplemental features which must be identified from machine to machine and used to your own advantage if your typing speed is to be increased.

The tab set and key, for example, if used properly, can increase your typing speed. Some typists insist that the tab key is a nuisance, and they prefer to use the space bar to check the alignment for a tab stop rather than use the automatic set on the typewriter. Others have the tab stop set every five characters or so and just tab across the page until they reach a spot relatively close to where they want to be and space or backspace until they hit the right spot. This is a waste of time! Set your tabs for each piece of correspondence, for each report, for each piece of tabulated material, and trust your machine. If the tab does not work properly, call your repair man.

For example, if you are typing material with a five-space indentation at the beginning of each paragraph, set the tab stop—one stroke of the tab stop does the same job as five strokes of the space bar. If anything you're typing calls for centering on the page, set the tab stop at the center and work from that point. This is especially necessary if you cannot move the carriage manually as is the case with some electric typewriters. The tab stops are a must for tabulated material. Words are simple, but numbers must be properly aligned:

North	45,352	14.01
South	3,846	4.65
East	68	.20
West	104,622	68.75

When the numbers are widespread, the tab stop may be set (as in the foregoing example) at the 100 mark, forward-spacing for numbers less than 100 and backspacing as appropriate for those in the 1,000's. Numbers to be aligned by decimal point may be handled similarly, setting the tab stop at the decimal and backspacing as required.

The margin sets can also be used to increase your typing speed; don't be reluctant to move them as necessary. Your margin sets will differ, depending upon the size of the paper you are using; obviously, the sets will vary depending upon whether you are typing on 8½ x 11 paper or a postcard. But suppose you are typing something with a lengthy quote (one or more paragraphs) which is to be indented equally on both sides. Reset the margins until you finish the quote, then return them to the first setting. This saves using the tab key at the beginning of each indented line and having to watch for the end of each line.

Another use for the margin set to increase your typing speed is in typing envelopes. Most addresses are at least three lines, and many are four or more. Even if you are typing a single envelope with a three-line address, you will save one stroke by using the margin set rather than the tab key (two movements to set and reset the margin, three to use the tab key for each line). If you are typing more than one envelope, figuring the number of strokes you save is a matter of arithmetic.

There are numbers on your typewriter which correspond to the number of spaces on your typing paper. For example, there are 102 elite spaces across an 8½" sheet of paper, and 12 elite spaces in one inch. If you are using a standard elite typewriter, therefore, you know that if the left side of the paper is set at "0", for a one-inch margin on either side, margin sets should be at 12 and 85 or 90—and for a two-inch margin on either side, they should be at 24 and 70 or 75. The right set will vary depending upon your typewriter and your own personal preference. Which brings up another feature that can be used to increase your typing speed: the bell. Every time you look up from your copy, you lose time. When the bell rings on your typewriter, you should know how many spaces are left on the line without having to look. You will know that you can type "at the" or "from him" before returning the carriage, and that "microanalytical" won't make it. Which brings up the question of hyphenating at the end of a line—necessary to preserve a uniform right-hand margin.

Every time you stop to look up a proper word division, you lose seconds of typing time. Remember that prefixes and suffixes can always be separated from the "stem" word, provided the prefix consists of at least two letters and the suffix consists of at least three. "E-vade" or "a-void" is not permitted, nor is "loving-ly" nor "accord-ed." Learn the prefixes and suffixes that can be properly divided from the stem and you will cut in half the time that is normally required to check the dictionary to be sure you are right. "Self" and "non", "un" and "in" can usually be separated, "ing and "tion" are suffixes which make a convenient dividing point.

Make a note of the numbers you need for various margin sets, such as 54 for typing envelopes which are 9½" wide (standard letter size), and 74 for those which are 12" wide. If you are typing columnar work, refer to the numbers to set up the task. For two columns, (for example, a list of names and addresses as they will appear on envelopes), you may want to type the left column, then reset the left margin to 55 for the right column. If your work is a list of names in the left column, with company affiliation in the right, set the tab stop at 55 and type across the page. A few minutes spent in thought and planning can increase your typing speed.

3. IMPROVE YOUR TYPING ACCURACY

Improve your typing accuracy and you will increase your net typing speed. You learned in school the importance of typing in rhythm, steadily rather than in spurts, and relaxed rather than tense. This is especially important if you have a prolonged typing assignment. Begin at a steady, almost leisurely pace, and you will be able to produce more copy over several hours than if you start at maximum speed, tense and determined to conclude the job at the earliest possible moment. With the latter approach, you will produce less in any given period of time than you will if you attack the assignment with a long-range viewpoint.

For example, you have a 12-hour typing job—no matter how hard you work, with the usual office interruptions, you will spend at least two days on it. If you type steadily and concentrate on avoiding tenseness and pushing yourself, you will make fewer errors (which will increase your net speed).

Typing is a skill that becomes, in time, automatic—in fact, almost *too* automatic. For example, we type without thinking, especially on routine material. Typing *accuracy* can be improved by practicing on unfamiliar material. If you're a medical secretary, practice typing legal documents; if you're in a credit office, practice typing from an engineering manual.

Even the best typist will make an occasional error, and the error must be corrected. Improving your typing accuracy will increase your typing speed because there are fewer errors to correct. There are many ways to correct typographical errors without using an eraser, but whatever means you use, be sure the correction is neat and as undetectable as possible. And by all means, be sure the correction is made on all *copies* of the material.

Assuming that your typing speed and accuracy are maximum, how is your productivity?

4. KNOW YOUR RATE OF PRODUCTIVITY

Time yourself on your various typing assignments so that you will have a reasonable estimate of the time that will be required to complete a particular task. Work out a chart for your own office, using Figure 6 as a guide. When you have your timing established, look for ways to cut the time required.

A personnel man once asked me how many pages of typing a good typist should produce during a work day. I asked, "Does she have to answer a telephone? Are there visitors to the office? How much time out does she have for lunch and coffee breaks? Is the typing 'straight' or technical? Are carbons required? Single- or double-spaced copy?" He threw up his hands.

Seldom is a secretary, or even a typist, able to work with no interruptions. You can increase the amount of work you produce by doing your part to hold the interruptions to a minimum. For example, handle telephone calls and visitors efficiently, but don't waste time in idle chatter; take your time out for lunch and coffee breaks, but take only the time allowed.

5. KNOW YOUR COMPANY PAPERS

If you use the simplified letter, you need worry only about the left and right margin sets; however, if you indent the date, complimentary close, or signature, note the proper tab

Typing Assignment	Time (Minutes)
Letters:	
Short letter from shorthand	10
transcribing machine	15
draft	8
Long letter from shorthand	20
transcribing machine	25
draft	15
Weekly sales report	30
Monthly statements	60
Weekly payroll	45
Double-spaced draft	8 (each page)
Double-spaced report (straight typing)	10 (each page)
(tabular or technical work)	15 (each page)

Figure 6. CHART OF TYPING PRODUCTIVITY—HOW LONG DOES IT TAKE? This is a work chart for a hypothetical job. Make up your own chart for the items peculiar to your office and compute your actual work time, subtracting interruptions such as telephone or intercom calls, or visitors to the office. For any of your work, count the time for preparation, including assembling carbon and second sheets, checking, proofreading, and correcting. If an envelope is required, count that as a part of preparing the finished product.

stop number and use that each time you type a letter. Follow the same rule for interoffice memoranda.

Take a few minutes to check your stationery to learn how many lines of typing you can get on one page. There are 66 lines of elite typing space on an 8½ x 11 sheet of paper (six lines per inch) but not all 66 lines are available for typing. Subtract six lines for a margin of at least one inch at the bottom of the page, the equivalent number of lines taken up by the company letterhead, the number of lines needed for the date, inside address, and signature, and the number of lines for a salutation and complimentary close if they are used. You will probably find that only about 30 lines are available for the body of the letter, and that includes double spacing between paragraphs. Learn to gauge your work, whether from shorthand notes or typed or handwritten copy, so that you know before you begin typing a letter whether it will fit on one page.

For double-spaced copy, you can get about 25 lines on an 8½ x 11 page of plain white bond, leaving ample margins at top and bottom.

If you have reports to type periodically, note the tab stops on a "dummy" (or a copy of a previous report). Put numbers in front of the columnar headings to indicate where typing is to begin and put numbers below to indicate where the tab stops are to be set.

6. TAKE ADVANTAGE OF GADGETS

There are many gadgets on the market that can help you increase your typing productivity. Sometimes these gadgets are given to secretaries by salesmen with office machines or supply companies as part of their promotional campaigns. Examples include a stick-on holder for the little pieces of treated paper used to "erase" typing errors; a ruler with typing spaces and lines indicated as well as inches, and available for either pica or elite type; and any number of products to simplify corrections, such as (in addition to the treated paper) liquid "paint," and self-correcting ribbons.

Modern typewriters have built-in indicators to show you how near you are to the end of the page. There is also a "backing sheet" with numbers on one side to indicate the number of lines remaining on the page. The best features of both are combined in one gadget described in the following section (see Figure 7 on page 68).

A PRACTICAL GADGET

You can make your own gadget, if you are willing to do a little arithmetic and set it up for your own typewriter, that will eliminate the guesswork about where you are on any given piece of paper. You know immediately whether you can get the complimentary close and typed signature and title on the first page, or whether you must save at least two lines of the letter to carry over to a second (or third) page. On a report, a news release, or any double-spaced copy, you know whether to shorten the page or include an additional line to avoid having a one-line portion of a paragraph at either the bottom or the top of the page.

Usually, a typewriter platen will be no more than 30 lines in circumference; some are less. On plain white paper, type a list of numbers [see Figure 7 (a)]. Trim the list of numbers so that the strip is between ¼ and ½ inch in width and cover it with transparent tape. Beginning with the number "30", stick the tape to the typewriter platen and roll the platen forward, keeping the numbers even on the edge of either the left or right side. The tape should overlap so that the number "1" is showing. Set the "1" for the last line of type on your paper to leave a one-inch margin. Do this by inserting a sheet of paper with a penciled line indicating the line which is one inch from the bottom of the page, release the paper bail, and roll the platen, holding the paper, until the number "1" is even with the penciled line. Engage the paper bail, and use the platen to roll the paper back until the sheet is released. At the exact point where the paper is released, note the number which is showing at the side of the platen—that is the number you can use any time you insert the same size paper and you will know, after approxi-

	Start typing to leave 1" margin at top	6	27
		5	26
		4	25
		3	24
		2	23
		1	22
35		24	21
34		23	20
33		22	19
32		21	18
31		20	17
30		19	16
29		18	15
28		17	14
27		16	13
26	For ⅓ page, start second section	15	12
25		14	11
24		13	10
23		12	9
22		11	8
21		10	7
20		9	6
19		8	5
18		7	4
17		6	3
16		5	2
15	Half page	4	1
14		3	27
13		2	26
12		1	25
11		24	24
10		23	23
9		22	22
8		21	21
7		20	20
6		19	19
5		18	18
4	For ⅓ page, start third section	17	17
3		16	16
2		15	15

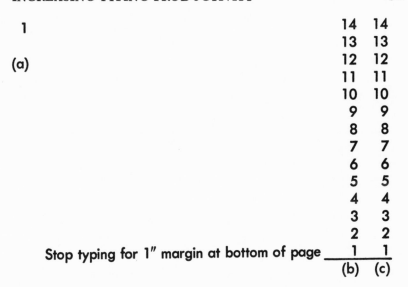

Figure 7. Vertical line spacer—a practical gadget. (a) To be taped to platen so that space No. 1 overlaps and appears on top. (b) Vertical spacing used on a Smith-Corona Electric Portable. (c) Vertical spacing used on an IBM Selectric. Numbers are for elite type.

mately two complete revolutions of the platen, exactly how many more lines you can type on the page and still leave a one-inch margin.

The usefulness of this gadget is unlimited. If you have a 12-line table to put on the page and only 10 lines available for typing, you know that the table will have to be put on the next page and you will have to include additional lines of text on the page you are typing. It works for double-spaced copy, too; with 10 lines left, you can get no more than five lines of double-spaced copy.

How to set up and type a report

There are many acceptable ways to set up a report; you should know at least one. Reports are generally double spaced with margins of at least one inch all the way around.

Preferred top margins are two inches when the page begins with a report or a chapter title, and one-and-a-half inches for other pages; the left margin should be one-and-a-half inches if the report is to be bound. The page number may be in the upper right corner, top center, or bottom center; but it must be at least one inch from the edge of the paper. If the first page is numbered (which is not necessary), the "1" is placed at bottom center regardless of how page 2 *et seq.* are numbered. To center horizontally, use the center of the *type line* rather than the center of the paper if right and left margins are unequal, as in a report to be bound.

A first order heading (name of report or chapter) should be centered and all caps; second order is centered, cap and lower case, and underscored; third order is flush with the left margin, cap and lower case, and underscored. Sub-headings under third order are best indented five spaces and numbered (1, 2, 3) or lettered (A, B, C). There should be three spaces between the last line of text and a new heading of any order, but only two spaces between the heading and the text following. Indent five spaces to indicate beginning of a paragraph.

In typed copy, whether single or double spaced, begin a new page with a new paragraph if possible; otherwise there must be no fewer than two lines of a paragraph at the bottom of a page and no fewer than two at the top of the next page. In a report, a heading of any order must be followed by at least two lines of text at the bottom of the page (don't leave the heading "dangling" with nothing under it). The margin must be *at least* one inch at the bottom of a page, but a wider margin may be left to avoid violation of this rule.

Titles of books and magazines may be typed as NEWSWEEK or *Newsweek*, but acceptable is simply Newsweek unless there is a possibility that the reader will not realize that this is the name of a publication. Works referred to by author may be in quotes: "The Scarlet Letter," by Hawthorne.

A general rule is to spell out numbers under 10, use numerals for those over 10. To be consistent, however, use 3, 15, and 27 (or two, five, and fifteen). Unless cents are included with dollars, leave off the decimal and zeros ($14 rather than

$14.00) when the material is informational only and not legal or contractual. Where two numbers are adjacent, one is usually written out and the other typed in numerals; e.g., eleven 20-minute sessions or 10 three-minute eggs.

How to set up and type an effective table

There are different types of tables and more than one way to prepare any of them. Any secretary should be able to type at least two kinds of tables, informal and formal, and should know at least one acceptable way to do each.

An informal table is one which contains itemized information, usually in the body of a letter or a report, which is centered and tabulated. It has no title and generally loses its usefulness if separated from the other material. An example of an informal table is:

The percentage of employees in the ABC organization, according to general work classification, can be estimated as follows:

Scientific and Technical	44.45%
Administrative and Clerical	52.25%
Service and Maintenance	3.30%

Spacing between the text and an informal table is one more than used in the text; i.e., the informal table is set off from single-spaced material by two spaces and from double-spaced material by three.

A formal table may be a single sheet of paper with no covering letter or memorandum to explain its purpose; it may be an enclosure to a letter or memorandum, a part of a report which contains other tables, or a part of an advertisement package. Regardless of its place within another document or its purpose as a solitary piece of information, the table should explain itself without any other substantiating piece of paper. That is, the table should present information which can be absorbed at a glance without further explanation either in a letter or an accompanying report.

A formal table has a title and may (but not necessarily) have a table number. A table title (including the table number, if any) is capped and centered; if there is more than one line in the title, which must be self-explanatory, it should be arranged in "inverted pyramid" style. A date may be included as a part of the title, but must appear somewhere on the page.

The table title may be underlined. To set off the table itself, double underlines may be used.

Columnar headings are essential. These should be determined to avoid repetition and/or to save space in the columns. The heading should "communicate" so that there is no question in the mind of the reader as to what the tabulation means.

The information may be arranged in almost any order, provided there *is* an order and the order makes sense. Some arrangements include: alphabetical order; by cost or size, in either ascending or descending order; by geographical area, type of material, color, or relationship of the items.

The vertical spacing within the tabulated information may be single or double, or a combination; e.g., single spacing by each group of two or more items and double spacing between the groups.

Horizontal spacing follows a definite pattern. Spacing between columns should be equal. To compute the number of spaces to allow between the columns, subtract the total number of spaces required for each column (the heading or the item, whichever requires more) from the total number of spaces in the line of type and divide the remainder by the number of columns minus one. If the number is greater than five, widen the margins on each side to reduce spaces between the columns to five or less.

A table is centered vertically as well as horizontally on the page. If there is a difference between the top and bottom margins, the top margin should be slightly wider.

Tips for proofreading rapidly and effectively

A written document should never be released in final form without having first been read to be sure it is correct. If an executive has dictated material for transcription, he may want to read the finished copy to be sure he said what he said the way he meant to say it, but he should never have to "proofread" material prepared for his signature, or release, for misspelled words, grammatical errors, or typographical mistakes—this is the secretary's responsibility.

One method of proofreading is done without assistance. The person responsible for the final typing is also responsible for the proofreading. If the material is "straight" typing so that a careful reading will point up any errors (such as a routine letter containing familiar words and phrases), the job is simple provided the proofreader is competent. The proofreader must be able to detect a transposition, a misspelled word or proper name, a grammatical error, or an error of omission (such as lack of indication of an enclosure, an incorrect list for distribution, or any error in a numeral whether in a date or a dollar amount). For example, even though the draft or shorthand has been read for errors before typing, it's always a good idea, if a meeting is set for Thursday, January 3, to check the calendar to be sure that January 3 *is* Thursday, rather than Wednesday or Friday. This is particularly important if there is a possibility that the author referred to the wrong calendar, a common error when material is prepared in one calendar year and the date referred to is in a different calendar year.

Absolutely unexcusable are the following types of proofreading errors: A letter addressed to Mr. F. C. Alley bears the salutation "Dear Mr. Allen"; a request to "please let me know which date world be convenient."

When proofreading material other than straight typing without assistance, following are some suggestions for proof-reading rapidly and effectively: First proofread against the draft to be sure that nothing has been omitted or overlooked.

When columns are numerical with totals for each column, one way to determine that each figure is correct is to add the columns on a machine—this is assuming that your typing is normally accurate and that you are equally accurate on the machine on which you add the figures. Another way to check tabulated material, particularly if it is technical or includes numbers, is to compare the draft with the final copy column by column, If there are a number of columns across the page which include non-numerical information, you may find it more efficient to take the draft copy and roll it around one finger of each hand, following the final copy line by line.

If you have several letters to type with the same message but different names, addresses, and salutations, check only the date, address, salutation, complimentary close, and notes such as enclosures and carbon copies; proofread the body of the letter from the previous letter typed. In other words, copy the body of each letter from the one previously typed, then compare the final letter with the draft. This assumes, of course, that you are alert enough *not* to copy the same error several times before you catch it.

If you proofread with another person, one reads and the other follows. Normally, the best procedure is for the reader to read from the draft and the follower to check the final copy. Unfamiliar words should be spelled out, any specification, symbols, or money amounts should receive special attention, and the follower (checking the final copy) should be sure that proper margins are observed and that any corrections are undetectable.

Chapter 5

AUTOMATED EQUIPMENT'S EFFECT ON THE SECRETARY AND OFFICE OPERATIONS

Business men and educators generally agree that automated equipment, while eliminating many jobs formerly performed by clerks and typists, will never replace the secretary. They also agree that the widespread use of automated equipment is changing, and will continue to modify, the secretarial job description.

Word processing centers, which are comparable to an automated secretarial pool, serve as a training ground for a correspondence secretary. In this area, the secretary is an expert in turning out perfect, typed copy. She knows her grammar, format, and style, knows how to edit and proofread, and can direct her professional future toward supervising the center.

The personal secretary, relieved of much of the routine typing responsibilities in her office, becomes an administrative secretary with more time to devote to assisting her executive and assuming more and more of his routine duties. She will not be completely divorced from her typewriter, because she will need to draft or compose material for him, she will type an urgent telegram or cable to be sent immediately, and she will continue to type his personal or confidential correspondence which he would prefer not to send to the center.

The administrative secretary, no longer chained to her typewriter, will be free to engage in the more responsible aspects of her job, such as arranging meetings; assembling portfolios of information needed for preparing reports or for attending conferences; making arrangements for business trips; abstracting reports or articles, gathering information, articles, or newspaper clippings for preparing speeches. Relieved of the pressure of extensive typing chores, she can be an effective public relations representative for her office by taking the time to deal graciously with all of her executive's associates.

The secretary in a small office or a small company will be less affected by automated operations. Sophisticated automated equipment is expensive and designed for extensive production. A small company does not have the volume of work in its office to justify its purchase, but rather will take advantage of centers which provide that kind of service on a rental basis. Therefore, its secretaries will continue their combination of administrative-correspondence duties, using conventional office equipment, but relieved of some of the routine and less interesting tasks that can be sent to an automated center.

Keeping up with advancing technology

An alert career secretary will not be the last to know about the latest developments in the field of automation, but one of the first. Automated equipment is the secretary's friend, not her enemy. A secretary is paid for her productivity, and with the help of the miraculous machinery available today, her productivity bears no relation to the "typewriter" of less than a hundred years ago.

At one time, within the memory of some of us, a typing speed of about 50 words a minute was considered very good on a manual machine and easy to maintain for a short time. However, an all-day typing job was exhausting because of the effort required to depress the keys. In addition to increasing the speed of the typist, today's electric machine is much less tiring to use, especially over a period of time.

Similar comparisons can be made with other types of office equipment. For example, the hand-crank adding maching grew into complicated electric calculators; now some electronic computers are so small they fit in your pocket.

These are examples of progress in the field of automation in the past; but despite the advances in technology that have made these machines a reality, there is more to come. You, as a career secretary, should keep abreast of the developments in new and improved office equipment and be knowledgeable enough to recommend to your executive, at the appropriate time, when to consider obtaining new equipment for your office.

Keeping up to date with the latest in office machinery and supplies

With improvements and changes in office machinery and supplies taking place so rapidly, how can you keep up with the latest developments? One way is to watch for advertisements in business magazines. The companies producing office machinery and supplies want the public to know about new and improved products, and one way to disseminate the information is to advertise.

Another way to keep up is to stay in touch with your salesmen. You'll find most salesmen eager to talk about their products and willing to discuss your individual needs. They will recommend what will be adequate without pressuring to sell a product that will be too sophisticated, or too expensive, for your office.

Periodically there will be exhibits of office machinery in your area and you will have an opportunity to see several different kinds and makes of equipment in one place. There are always representatives to demonstrate the equipment and to permit you to try it out for yourself if you wish. Meetings of professional business associations usually have exhibits of office machinery and supplies; for example, meetings sponsored by the National Secretaries Association (International).

Assume that you have heard about, or seen at some exhibit, a piece of office equipment you believe would increase the efficiency of your office. First you should gather as much written information as you can, such as brochures, advertisements, or articles, then discuss the matter with your executive. If he agrees that your suggestion should be investigated further, contact your salesman. In most cases a salesman will bring and set up in your own office the equipment under consideration. He will demonstrate the operation to both you and your executive, and may leave it with you for a week or two so that you may use it on a trial basis. New typing or dictating equipment, for example, may seem strange and awkward at first and hardly worth the trouble to learn to operate. However, by practicing with it for several days, you will be better able to assess its value to your office operations.

While the shorthand pad or shorthand machine is still essential in many areas, the executive and the secretary frequently prefer to use dictating and transcribing equipment. For the executive, this means he can dictate either in or away from the office, at home or on an airplane, or in a hotel room following a conference or meeting while the business at hand is fresh in his mind. He can make more effective use of his time in the office, scheduling appointments and phone calls throughout the day with no need to allow an extended period for direct dictation to his secretary.

The secretary has more time and more freedom in scheduling her own work day. She has an opportunity to devote more of her time to administrative duties and to consider ways to improve the efficiency of her office. And if the amount of transcription on the machine is excessive, she can turn it over to an assistant or to a word processing center.

To keep up with the latest in office supplies, in addition to depending upon your salesman for advice, take advantage of advertisements of new products which offer free samples. Frequently, to introduce a new product, a company will include in its advertisement a section to be clipped, filled in, and returned to obtain a free sample to try in your office. Free samples are usually offered when the product is relatively inexpensive.

Your new typewriter—a problem of selection

When a secretary goes into an office for the first time, she usually inherits the office equipment already there. The time will come, however, when there will be the question of replacing a worn out or obsolete typewriter. Most executives, once the price range has been determined, will leave to the secretary the decision as to the make and model of typewriter to be purchased.

Follow these rules for reaching any decision: get the facts, analyze the data, list available alternatives, then make your selection. Typewriters come in all sizes, styles, and colors, and range from the very simple to the extremely complex. Determine your needs, investigate the models which appear to meet those needs, and present your recommendation to your executive with the reasons for your choice.

If your typing consists primarily of correspondence, invoices, forms, bills, or other items no larger than letter-size paper, an electric portable may be your most efficient purchase. This type of machine is relatively inexpensive, quite durable, and offers a choice of type styles and special keys. The carriage length is sometimes limited, however, and it lacks some of the features found in larger machines.

There is a typewriter that will fit your needs, however sophisticated they may be. There are interchangeable carriages so that you have a long carriage when you need it, otherwise you may use a shorter one. There are interchangeable keys if you need them for typing technical materials or foreign languages.

The most important consideration in the selection of your typewriter is to be sure you obtain one that will be adequate for your office over the next few years, because a typewriter is a very durable piece of office equipment and will last almost indefinitely if properly cared for. Don't overlook the possibility of a "new" used typewriter. A good rebuilt typewriter will give years of service and costs much less than a new one.

Of equal importance is to choose the equipment with the features you need, but don't invest company money on extras that will never be used. Remember that typing equipment can range in price from about a hundred dollars to several thousands.

Care for your typewriter as though it were your own, because it is. A service contract is a good investment because it guarantees regular checkups by a competent service man; this is preventive maintenance. If you do not have a service contract for your machine, your own responsibility for caring for it is increased. Follow the manufacturer's directions for daily care and cleaning (or check your secretarial handbook for general directions) and arrange for a periodic cleaning and inspection by a reputable repairman.

How to type 150 words a minute without touching the keyboard

Even though your average typing speed is 65 words a minute, you can type 150 words a minute or more without touching the keyboard—again. Automatic typewriters are the answer for secretaries with routine correspondence or reports to prepare regularly.

Magnetic cards or tapes, depending upon the type of machine, can be prepared in one typing and used over and over again, inserting only additions or corrections as needed, and adding the variable material such as name and address. The typewriter can be programmed to type forms, invoices, purchase orders, etc., as well as letters, memoranda, and reports. The automatic typewriter also can be used for conventional typing, that is, the same as any typewriter without automatic features.

Although a good secretary will have no difficulty in learning to operate an automatic typewriter, she may find it more efficient to attend a formal school for at least a few days to be sure she will achieve maximum efficiency on the machine in minimum time.

Some automatic typewriters can be tied into a computer. Material to be prepared in draft form for revision and editing, perhaps not once but several times, need be typed only once on this equipment. Manuscripts, technical papers, speeches, special reports, legal documents and the like, any material that must be meticulously composed, revised, and edited so that the final copy is as perfect as it can be made by those responsible for its production, are ideal for this type of machine. A secretary types a very rough draft one time, including directions to the computer, and gets back perfect copy ready for revision and editing. Subsequently, only revisions and corrections need be fed into the computer, and each time perfect copy is returned.

Hours can be spent in typing a lengthy report, for example, and the computer can provide finished copy in a matter of seconds. Computerized automatic typewriters can perform such instant miracles as centering a title or heading, centering and properly spacing a table, justifying margins, deleting or adding a line or a paragraph anywhere in the text, or moving sentences or paragraphs from one section to another.

How to select the most efficient reproduction method and equipment for the job at hand

Whether you have reproduction facilities in your own office or organization or whether you use an outside agency for multiple copies, you should be aware of the comparative costs of the methods and equipment available. The least expensive method of reproduction for a limited number of copies is the carbon copy. In most cases, up to ten readable carbon copies can be obtained using an electric typewriter and good quality second sheets and carbon paper.

Almost every business office includes a copy machine as a part of its standard equipment. Remember, however, the cost per page with a copy machine is about five times the cost of a carbon copy; don't use the copy machine to reproduce two or three copies of an original letter just because you don't like to make carbons.

Check with the head of your reproduction department or your local printer to determine the most efficient way to reproduce multiple copies. You'll find that the "prettier" the job, the more expensive it is; therefore, sacrifice beauty for quick service and dollar savings by selecting the less expensive method, especially for a relatively small number of copies. For copies in the hundreds and above, such as a brochure describing the company's products, you will want to investigate the more expensive methods, including different type styles, color illustrations or photographs, etc. The decision, of course, is your executive's; your responsibility is to give him enough information to make the correct one.

Cooperate with automated equipment, and it will cooperate with you

If you are using automated equipment, either in your own office or in a center outside your office or your company, your responsibility is to see that the information fed into the machine is correct and understandable by the machine and/or the operator. An automated typewriter, for example, is no better than its operator; and a poor typist is a poor "word processor," or correspondence secretary.

Assuming that your instructions are properly given and the machine is properly operated, how pleasant life can be for you when you can spend an hour "setting up" a job and get back a week's work the following day! An example is a letter of invitation to each of 50 speakers to participate in a symposium and present a talk on a certain day and at a certain time. One letter can be prepared, leaving addresses, salutations, subject of the talk, time, and day to be filled in. "The "form" part of the letter need be proofread only once; then only the differences in each need be checked.

Learn how to cooperate with automated equipment, and when and how to use it, and you will find it will cooperate with you—eliminating many tedious typing chores for you.

Getting ready for conversion to the metric system

Although we may find it difficult to think in terms of getting so many kilometers to the liter of gasoline, our country is preparing to convert to the metric system, which is used throughout most of the world. We may enjoy weighing 60 kilograms instead of 132 pounds, but many enjoy less measuring 60 centimeters at the waist.

Since we are not likely to have much influence on the decision as to if or when we convert to the metric system, we can only be ready for it. For a quick calculation of conversion from English to metric measurements, or vice versa, you may want to get a "calculator" which operates something like a slide rule.* It's very easy to use and is, in fact, within the grasp of children in elementary school. For your ready reference, Figure 8 on page 84 lists some of the conversion equivalents.

---

*May be obtained from Union Carbide Corporation, Educational Aids Department, P. O. Box 363, Tuxedo, NY 10987.

CONVERSION EQUIVALENTS

DISTANCE

ENGLISH TO METRIC

1 Inch = 2.5 Centimeters (Cm)
1 Foot = .3048 Meter (M)
1 Yard = .9144 Meter (M)
1 Mile = 1.609 Kilometers
5 Miles = 8.045 Kilometers
10 Miles = 16.094 Kilometers
20 Miles = 32.187 Kilometers
30 Miles = 48.281 Kilometers
40 Miles = 64.375 Kilometers
50 miles = 80.468 Kilometers
60 Miles = 96.562 Kilometers
70 Miles = 112.655 Kilometers
80 Miles = 128.750 Kilometers
90 Miles = 144.843 Kilometers
100 Miles = 160.936 Kilometers
Nautical Mile = 1852 Meters

(1 Statute Mile = 0.8689 Nautical Miles)

METRIC TO ENGLISH

1 Centimeter = 2/5 Inch
1 Meter = 39 Inches (1.1 Yds.)
1 Hectometer = 109.36 Yards
1 Kilometer = 5/8 or .62 Mile
5 Kilometers = 3.1 Miles
10 Kilometers = 6.2 Miles
20 Kilometers = 12.4 Miles
30 Kilometers = 18.6 Miles
40 Kilometers = 24.9 Miles
50 Kilometers = 31.1 Miles
60 Kilometers = 37.3 Miles
70 Kilometers = 43.5 Miles
80 Kilometers = 49.7 Miles
90 Kilometers = 55.9 Miles
100 Kilometers = 62.1 Miles
1 Kilometer = .544 Nautical Miles

CAPACITY

ENGLISH TO METRIC

1 Cubic Inch = 16.387 Cu. Cnt.
1 Cubic Foot = 0.0283 Cu. Meter
1 Cubic Yard = 0.7645 Cu. Meter
1 Pint = 0.4732 Liter
1 Quart:2 Pints = 0.9463 Liter
1 Gallon:4 Qts. = 3.7853 Liters

METRIC TO ENGLISH

1 Cubic Cm. = 0.0610 Cu. Inch
1 Liter = 2.1134 Pints
1 Hectoliter = 26.4180 Gallons
1 Cubic Meter = 1.3079 Cu. Yards

1 English Gallon = 1.200 U.S. Gallons = 4.5460 Liters
1 U.S. Gallon = 0.833 English Gallon = 3.7854 Liters
1 Liter = 0.220 English Gallon = 0.2642 U.S Gallon

METRIC TO ENGLISH (Liquid)

1/2 Liter = Approx. 1 Pint
1 Liter = 1.06 Quarts
2 Liters = 2.11 Quarts
4 Liters = 1.05 (.88) *Gallon
8 Liters = 2.11 (1.76) Gallons
10 Liters = 2.64 (2.2) Gallons
15 Liters = 3.96 (3.3)* Gallons
20 Liters = 5.28 (4.4) Gallons
30 Liters = 7.92 (6.6) Gallons
40 Liters = 10.56 (8.8) Gallons
50 Liters = 13.21 (11) Gallons
100 Liters = 26.42 (22) Gallons

*British Imperial Gallons shown in parentheses.

WEIGHT

ENGLISH TO METRIC

1 Grain = 0.065 Grams
1 Ounce = 28.35 Grams
1 Pound = 453.592 Grams
1 Short Ton = 907.18 Kilograms
1 Long Ton = 1,016.06 Kilograms

METRIC TO ENGLISH

1 Gram = 15.4 Grains
28 Grams = 1 Ounce
1 Kilogram = 2.2 Pounds
20 Kilograms = 44 Pounds
40 Kilograms = 88.2 Pounds

TEMPERATURE

FAHRENHEIT TO CELSIUS

+212° = +100°
+194° = + 90°
+176° = + 80°
+158° = + 70°
+140° = + 60°
+122° = + 50°
+104° = + 40°
+ 86° = + 30°
+ 68° = + 20°
+ 50° = + 10°
+ 41° = + 5°
+ 32° = 0°
+ 23° = − 5°
+ 14° = − 10°
+ 5° = − 15°
0° = − 17.8°
− 4° = − 20°
− 13° = − 25°
− 22° = − 30°
− 31° = − 35°
− 40° = − 40°

To Compute Fahrenheit
Multiply Celsius by 1.8, add 32

To Compute Celsius
Subtract 32 from Fahrenheit and divide by 1.8

° F = (°C 9/5) + 32

Figure 8. Conversion equivalents—be ready for the metric system.

Chapter 6

PRACTICAL SUGGESTIONS FOR PREPARING YOUR EXECUTIVE'S CORRESPONDENCE

THE MANAGER WHO WRITES AN EFFECTIVE LETTER (one which has the proper tone to promote or to retain good will, and communicates) accomplishes his purpose. Even if the communication is properly worded, a carelessly prepared letter creates a poor impression on the reader before he reaches the salutation, if there is one, regardless of what the message is. On the other hand, the reader receives a favorable impression the moment he unfolds the letter if it is attractively done. The suggestions on the following pages may be of help to you in preparing your executive's business correspondence.

Creating the proper impression
through business correspondence

Your job is to be sure your executive's artistic word picture is artistically framed and that the typing is letter-perfect. Any necessary typing corrections are undetectable, words are divided properly at the end of a line to keep a relatively even right margin, and the letter is properly framed on the page. For ease of reading, a five-inch line is recommended—with margins of about 1½ inches on either side.

A letter of no more than one page is preferred. If you can hold the letter to one page by using a line longer than five inches (margins of not less than one inch on each side), then do so. The trend in business letter writing today is to save money, time, and effort without sacrificing the primary purpose of getting the job done. Try to avoid a letter with a second page consisting of one line, a signature, and the distribution list. If space permits, put the typed signature at the bottom of the page, and place the dictator's and typist's initials in the top right-hand corner with the distribution list beneath. Typing the distribution list on the first page works well on a letter of two pages or more, as well. This saves turning to page 2 or 3 to see whose copy you have or who is on the distribution list.

Much attention has been given to the "attention" line. Direct address is normally preferred, but there are times when your letter gets quicker results when you address it to the company or organization, attention of an individual or office. If the person normally responsible is away from the office, his assistant will probably attend to the matter.

The U. S. Postal Service prefers that an attention line be done this way:

AMATEUR APPLIANCE COMPANY
ATTN: MR. J. M. COOK, VICE PRESIDENT
P. O. BOX 1235
KNOXVILLE, TN 37916

If you use a salutation, it may be either "Dear Sir," "Gentlemen," or "Dear Mr. Cook."

The subject line is another controversial point in placement within the letter (before or after the salutation). Regardless of where it appears, a subject line serves a very useful purpose to both the sending and the receiving office. It's helpful both in locating previous correspondence and in filing. The subject line is indicated by its placement within the letter and is preferably all caps; there is no need to waste time and effort by typing "Subject:" "In Re:" or "Re:" If there is a notation on a letter "In reply refer to: ABC:DE/fg 327," then the subject line in your reply might read as follows:

ABC:DE/fg 327 YOUR ORDER NO. XH 32975 FOR WANG CALCULATORS

You may also use cap and lower case with underlining for the subject.

If a letter is more than one page, second (and continuing) page headings are very important. If the second page is separated from the first, the heading should enable you to identify and reassemble the complete letter. This applies to both incoming and outgoing correspondence. Notations on page 2 *et seq.* may be made using this form:

To Acme Chemical Co.   **2**   **6/15/78**

or this one:

> **To Mr. Carver**
> **Page 2**
> **6/15/78**

Some executives elect to eliminate the initials of the dictator and typist on the original letter, whether or not they are shown on the carbons or office copies. If they are used, the dictator's initials appear first, the typist's following. In general the notation ABC:DEF:gh would mean that the letter, which is signed by ABC, was prepared by DEF at the direction of ABC and typed by gh who is probably DEF's secretary.

Special handling, including airmail, special delivery, registered or insured mail, etc., should be above the address and separated by a single space. For example,

AIRMAIL

Mr. John Z. Jones, President
QRX Company, P. O. Box 1
Seattle, WA 98703

A good idea is to type the envelope first, and then the letter. In that way you give your full attention to the address on the envelope, and double check it to be sure it is correct and that any special notice has been given to the U. S. Postal Service. Be sure the complete address on the letter is the same as the one on the envelope. By indicating above the address the special handling requested, your office and any other receiving copies of the correspondence will have a record of how the letter was posted.

If you show your carbon copies above or below the enclosures, which way means the people on the distribution list did or did not receive the enclosures? To be sure that everybody knows who got the enclosures and who did not, simply note it and it won't make any difference *where* you put your distribution list:

cc: John Doe w/enclosure
Richard Roe w/o enclosure

And the distribution list is never wrong if it is in simple alphabetical order. This saves trying to guess at the proper protocol as to whose name should appear first in order of rank within the company.

For years we have used "cc" to mean carbon copy and "bc" to mean "blind" copy, or the recipient of the "bc" is not shown on the original of the letter. More recently, however, "cc" is used to indicate copies made by other than carbon copy; for example, ditto, mimeograph, multilith, printing, etc. Another notation in vogue is "pc" for photocopy or "xc" for Xerox copy. Whatever method you choose, unless there is a good reason to keep the distribution list a secret, list the recipients of copies on the original document; in any case, list them on all copies within your organization. Then each individual on the distribution list will know who has the information and whether further distribution within his area of responsibility is necessary.

However the copies for distribution are reproduced, make at least one carbon copy for your own office. Examples of what may happen when you type the original only and trust a copy machine: (1) executive extracts original from typewriter, signs it, hands it to the Sales Manager who is already late for his plane, and then asks you for a copy (which you don't have); (2) copy machine isn't working and the four-page letter must be mailed immediately; (3) machine is making poor copies, and soon the first two paragraphs are smeared and unreadable—in effect, no copy available.

Suggested letter styles

There are a number of standard letter styles. Your executive's preference will determine the style you use unless he permits you to choose your own.

The trend in business letter writing today is to save money, time, and effort. The block style, illustrated on the following page, follows this form:

June 15, 1978

Mr. John Doe
P. O. Box 25
Oasis, UT   84650

Dear Mr. Doe:

Thank you for your invitation to participate. . . .

Sincerely yours,

Henry Ferguson
Sales Manager

The streamlined block form is the simplified letter which omits the salutation and complimentary close and follows this form:

June 15, 1978

Mr. John Doe
P. O. Box 25
Oasis, UT   84650

Thank you, John, for your invitation to participate. . . .

Henry Ferguson
Sales Manager

The modified block is still another form:

July 15, 1978

Mr. John Doe
P. O. Box 25
Oasis, UT   84650

Dear Mr. Doe:

Thank you for your invitation to participate. . . .

Sincerely yours,

Henry Ferguson
Sales Manager

A further shortening of the business letter can be illustrated by the memorandum form which may be the same as the simplified letter or the modified block with the salutation and complimentary close omitted; this form, however, does not stress the use of a name at the beginning and end of the message. Some organizations follow the normal memorandum form (i.e., omit the address) when the communication is sent to one with whom there is much correspondence on a regular basis. Regular company letterhead is used, but the form is:

To John Doe   Date: July 15, 1978

Thanks for your invitation—I'll be there on Monday at 10:00 a.m.

Henry Ferguson

or any other acceptable memorandum form, with or without a subject.

A style we see seldom in this country today is indented with closed punctuation, but it is still used outside the United States. The letter might be prepared abroad in this way:

June 15, 1978

Mr. John Doe
  P. O. Box 25,
    Oasis, Utah, U.S.A.

Dear Mr. Doe:

Thank you for your invitation to participate. . . .

Sincerely yours,

Henry Ferguson,
Sales Manager.

The simplified letter appeals to the people who contend that a business letter is not necessarily addressed to a "dear" one, and that the sender is not "yours," sincerely or otherwise. Some executives prefer "Dear John," but they prefer "Cordially" or "Sincerely," omitting the "yours."

Your executive will have his own letter style, whether archaic or modern, or one uniquely his own. He may use a conventional mode of address, salutation, and complimentary close on routine correspondence, but express "himself" on personal notes or letters to friends or close business associates.

An executive in Washington, D. C., has his own unique style of writing a business letter. A letter from him might be done in this manner:

Mr. John Doe
P. O. Box 25
Oasis, UT   84650

I am delighted, John Doe, that you can meet me for lunch on Tuesday, June 23. . . .

Cordially,

Richard Roe

He uses no salutation, but does use a complimentary close (without being "yours"). He writes the way he talks, and his personality comes through on paper as effectively as it does in person.

A member of the faculty of Denison University has his own style of writing and communicates in his own inimitable way. His letter might read like this:

Mr. John Doe
P. O. Box 25
Oasis, UT   84650

John,

Call me when you get the report of your grade for this semester. Things may look glum now, but a cheery thought is that there is plenty of room for improvement. You can do it, and I'll help any way I can.

Hang tough,

Ron Winters

Your executive may be the conservative type who prefers something like this:

My dear Doe:

It is my pleasure to learn that you can meet me for lunch on Tuesday, June 23. . . .

Respectfully yours,

Whatever your executive's preference, do it that way. Don't worry if you can't find an example "in the book"—it's your business to please him. And if his preference is a bit different, learn to live with it; different is not necessarily wrong.

How to help your executive prepare his correspondence

Perhaps there is no more explicit way that a secretary can prove her value to her executive than her assistance in preparing necessary correspondence. Assume that an inquiry has come into the office for certain information, some of which is available in your own files, and a part of which must be obtained from another office. Assemble what you can from your own file, request as much as you can from other offices within your organization, and draft a summary of the information you have been able to collect.

Routinely attach to incoming mail pertinent prior correspondence, files, or your own notes which will permit him to have at his fingertips all information available to you concerning the matter. If you can determine, reviewing the information that you yourself can readily obtain, that additional information will be of help, you will obtain it, if possible, before putting the correspondence across his desk. For example, a customer writes that he can be in your office at 9:00 a.m. on Thursday, and will you please make a hotel reservation for him for the evening of Wednesday, late arrival? Make the reservation and attach a note to the correspondence; it's much easier to cancel a reservation on long notice than to make a suitable one on short notice.

Another example: A customer writes that he would like to meet with your executive and the Sales Manager any morning next week, any time before noon. A simple telephone call to the Sales Manager's office will ascertain if there is one time more convenient than another for him, and if there is any time when he will not be available for a meeting—this small effort on your part will save your executive the need to check the Sales Manager's schedule; all he will need be concerned with is his own.

When and how to correct grammatical errors
in business correspondence

Whether your executive dictates to you personally or to a machine or writes his own draft, he is concerned primarily with communicating. That is, he wants the addressee to "get the message." He is prone to dictate or write as he speaks, not the way an English grammarian would do it. Your responsibility is to see that his message is transmitted correctly with regard to grammar.

This assumes, of course, that *you* know grammar, and that you know where to look for help with a grammatical problem. You will find information on grammar in a dictionary, a secretarial handbook, or an English handbook. Slips in grammar most frequently made by executives occur in the area of subject-verb agreement. In the foregoing sentence, for example, no executive would say or write "slips is made," but when the subject is widely separated from the verb, he may make such an error without realizing it—"Slips in grammar most frequently made by an executive occurs in the area of subject-verb agreement." To correct such slips, you must be able to identify both the subject and the verb in the sentence.

No secretary worth the position would permit any written work to leave her office with a misspelled word in it. Unless you are absolutely certain that a word is spelled correctly, look it up! And look it up before you type it by guess—the seconds required to check beforehand may prevent a correction if you have guessed wrong.

More difficult words to spell correctly are those which sound alike but have different spellings for different meanings. Beware of, and double check, such sound-alikes as principal-principle, counsel-council, accept-except, affect-effect, to mention a few of the most common.

Know your vocabulary! Don't use a flagrantly wrong word: If you are requesting a biographical sketch, don't ask for a bibliography; don't confuse personnel with personal (a personnel office, a personal shopper).

General usage often causes a change in whether something is considered gramatically right or wrong. For example, it is no longer a cardinal sin to split an infinitive or to end a sentence with a preposition. Unless your executive expects you to edit his work extensively, don't. Prepare your executive's written work verbatim, if that is his wish, making only minor corrections that he will be unable to detect.

On the other hand, if you are permitted to "clean up" his dictation or rough draft, watch for hackneyed expressions or clichés and shorten them. An executive who likes to "enclose herewith" is usually reluctant to part with the "herewith," but educate him. Substitute short words for involved expressions which mean the same thing; for example,

if = in the event that
now = at the present time, or at this time

Check the grammar section of your reference books for other lengthy phrases which can be effectively shortened.

Your responsibility for business papers prepared by others for your executive's signature

When someone else prepares a letter or memorandum for your executive's signature, presumably the secretary has checked it for typographical or grammatical errors—but don't take it for granted. As you would any piece of correspondence originating in your office, read it carefully both for content and for errors. Remember that in many cases correspondence is the only impression a customer/client will ever have concerning your executive and your company. Check it as carefully as you do your own work: Check for the proper distribution of copies, if any; whether special handling is required and, if so, if it is noted on both the letter and the envelope; whether enclosures are indicated and are included with the package. If the letter passes your inspection, it is ready for the executive.

However, if you find an error of either commission or omission, exercise judgment in the way the correction is to be made. That is, correct or retype the letter yourself, return it to the typist, or give it to your executive with the errors noted. The latter would be best if he is likely to have additional changes to make.

If your executive is expected to sign a transmittal for a report which has been prepared in another office, check only the correspondence. The office preparing the report is responsible for the accuracy of the information it contains.

Although your executive is not required to sign or approve immediately a document sent across his desk, you may want to "tickle" him with a gentle reminder if it is not dispatched within a reasonable time. This is not to chide him for the delay (there may be a good reason for his failure to release it), but merely to be sure it has not been inadvertently buried in the other papers on his desk.

Chapter 7

ACCOMPLISHING MORE
WITH LESS EFFORT
THROUGH PRACTICAL
ORGANIZATION OF WORK

YOU MAY KNOW A SECRETARY WHO FLITS ABOUT with hair flying, no makeup, racing down the hall breathlessly with a handful of disheveled papers—always behind in her work, and always harassed and frustrated by the unfinished work at the end of the day. You may also know a secretary who always looks like a fashion model, even at the end of the day, with never a hair out of place, makeup always perfect, unhurried, pleasant and cheerful; her office the "wide-area" effect with no jumbled stacks of papers on the desk or filing cabinet, whatever the time of the day.

The difference is organization.

How to plan your work to keep on schedule during a normal work day

Some jobs must be scheduled ahead as much as several weeks, months, or even years. Agendas are a big help—an agenda for each day of the week, one for each month, one for each quarter, one on a semiannual or annual basis. Write down, realistically, what must be done each day of the week or month, allowing time for telephone calls, visitors, or crash jobs for your executive, but set for yourself an *achievable* goal for the day. Then set about accomplishing each day's objective in a methodical, well-planned way.

Some days the telephone is compassionately considerate—but other days it may ring constantly. Sometimes visitors will come in and out of the office in a steady stream, and other days you will be almost uninterrupted by callers. A crisis (and one should happen seldom, not every five minutes) must be dealt with on the spot, but anything unusual, other than a genuine crisis, should not disrupt your planned schedule.

Figure 9 is a sample daily schedule for a secretary. If your executive has a scheduled time for dictation, this should be added; however, he will probably require your attention on an intermittent basis throughout the day, and his needs always come first. Note that in addition to serving as a guide to what to do and when, the work schedule also can be used as a checklist to make sure that nothing has been overlooked. This is also a useful piece of paper to hand to a substitute when you're away from the office.

Determine a day in advance, if possible, what your routine for the next day should be: Handling the incoming mail, initiating or answering telephone calls, dictation and other personal duties for your executive, greeting and assisting visitors in the office, etc. Special projects must be worked into the routine. If information is to be collected from several offices, you must decide which would be most efficient—to telephone your request or to send a memorandum to the several people involved.

8:30 – 9:00	Coffee Check Executive's out box Check calendar for Executive's schedule Office housekeeping
9:00 – 11:00	Executive's time (dictation and discussion) Yesterday's unfinished business Outgoing mail
11:00	Mail pickup and delivery
11:00 – 12:00	Incoming mail
12:00 – 1:00	Lunch
1:00 – 3:00	Correspondence Outgoing mail
3:00	Mail pickup and delivery
3:00 – 3:10	Coffee
3:10 – 4:30	Incoming mail Reports and projects Check tickler file
4:30 – 5:00	Office housekeeping Filing

Figure 9. SAMPLE DAILY WORK SCHEDULE

If the information is needed at once, telephoning may be best—
if you have enough advance notice, a written request with a
stated deadline will help you to schedule your work for, say, a
week from Wednesday.

If you have a routine job every Friday which requires two hours, plus or minus a few minutes, include that in your daily agenda for Friday. The important consideration is to set for yourself a goal of accomplishment which can be achieved within the standard eight-hour day. If your goal is too low, that is, if you complete your self-assigned work in less than eight hours, you are not setting your goal high enough. If your goal is too high and you fail to achieve it, either your estimation of your own capability is too high or you have not allowed the necessary time for unanticipated interruptions

Why every good secretary should be a clock-watcher

The term "clock-watcher" has a negative connotation for most people since it implies that the clock-watcher is eagerly awaiting the time for a coffee break, lunch, or the quitting whistle. However, there is a positive connotation for the secretary. A good secretary is a good clock-watcher. She knows when the morning mail will be delivered and when the outgoing mail must be in the out-box to be postmarked the day it has been dispatched. She must know to the minute when certain information must be ready for a meeting of the Board of Directors or the sales staff. She must know when letters and memoranda for her executive's signature must be ready so that he will have time to read and sign them before he leaves the office for an out-of-town trip.

You must watch the clock to keep up with appointments for your executive. If he has an appointment at 11:00 with someone you've never seen, it will help you to know that a stranger who shows up in your office around 11:00 is probably the expected visitor. And even though you have your executive's calendar marked with his daily schedule, you may need to remind him to look at it to keep him reasonably close to the schedule he has planned for himself.

Watching the clock is essential if you are to keep to your own pre-planned daily schedule. It will point up necessary adjustments when your work load shifts or when it is obvious that you are allowing too much time for one operation and not enough for another. Don't panic if you have not cleared your desk before the end of the day. Routine reports or correspondence and perhaps other things as well can simply be incorporated in the next day's schedule—or the next week's depending upon the urgency. The important thing is to watch the clock to be sure you are performing each day at maximum efficiency.

How to assign your own priorities

Your executive's interests come first. Assign your priorities with no thought as to which is easier or quicker, but which is more important to him. He may indicate to you certain tasks which he prefers to be done first, but if not, you must use your own judgment. Assume that he enters the office in a rush, pitches his hat on the rack, and barks "Get Smith on the telephone, I'm going to Chicago, see if you can get me on the 10:00 flight this morning, and bring your book." Assuming you are reasonably alert, you will "get Smith" first to occupy your executive while you check his requested reservations. Hopefully, when he has finished talking with Smith, you can report that his reservations are confirmed and "bring your book" for dictation.

With a beginning like this, which you should know to expect, then you may settle down to assigning your own priorities. Usually, it's a good idea to keep your executive occupied with telephone calls while you send telegrams and cables, type an urgent letter, or make or cancel an appointment. In case he has forgotten that a letter or memorandum requires an answer immediately, remind him of it—even if it means a lengthy session of dictation or a lengthy typing project.

When your executive is out of town, you can revise your daily schedule and use the time allotted to him to catch up and be ready for his return. You should have your own work divided into priority groups, in 1, 2, 3 order, and of course do the top priority group first. Don't put a disagreeable task on the bottom of the stack (it has a habit of coming to the top periodically); in fact, it's a good idea to put the disagreeable tasks on top—when you get rid of them, you can enjoy completing the rest of the work.

Even when your executive is not in the office, his interests have top priority. The incoming mail, a telephone call, a visitor to the office, anything affecting your executive's responsibilities or the company profit margin takes precedent over your own planned schedule. Don't worry if you fail to complete all the tasks you planned while he was away; a good secretary is quite often more valuable to her executive when he is away from the office than when he is there.

How to remember to keep your promises

How irritating it is to have someone respond to a nudge for information requested previously with "I'm sorry, I forgot!" The recipient of such an excuse has no alternative but to assume that the excuser considered the request unimportant or, even worse, the requester unimportant. Don't be an excuser—write it down! Write it down and put your note where you will find it at the appropriate time. For example, you answer the telephone and Mr. Smith leaves a message for your executive to call "when he returns to the office." You make a note and put it either with his material of first priority when he returns to the office or on your own calendar with telephone calls to be returned at his convenience.

If a request is made to you to supply information that

is normally your responsibility, be realistic and promise the information by a specific time. "I'll call you back in a few minutes," "I can get that for you by noon tomorrow," or "I'll have that by the first of the month." Make a note, follow through, and keep your promise!

How to plan ahead to meet deadlines on time

If information is required by a certain time, determine how long it will take you to accumulate the necessary data, and begin far enough in advance to meet the deadline without a last-minute crisis. Assume a request comes into your office on February 1 to compare the sales records of 17 districts in the southwest for the period ending December 31, and the information is requested by March 15. Your executive, if left to his own devices, may put the paper on his "to do" schedule for March 15, and therein may develop a crisis. You should note this request on your calendar and, if you assume that two weeks will be required to accumulate the necessary information, remind him, not later than March 1, if he has done nothing up to that point.

If you know a certain report is due on the 15th of each month, determine how much time will be required to accumulate the necessary information, how long it will take you to consolidate it, and how much time you will need to type it. Then you simply back up from the time it is due, and begin the process of preparing it the requisite time in advance—always allowing a percentage of time for contingency.

For example, if you anticipate that it will require seven working days to accumulate the information, two working days to consolidate it, and four hours to type it, request your information ten working days before the due date, "tickle" the requestees five days before the due date (remembering that too many people look at the deadline as the date to start worrying about the request), and hopefully you will receive what you need in time to complete your assignment to meet your own deadline.

How and when to delegate jobs
to increase your output

Suppose you are a secretary to a middle-rank supervisor with no assistance in your own office. How, then, can you delegate jobs when there is no delegatee? Look for possibilities among your peers. You may find one or more of your co-workers who will agree to lend you a helping hand in exchange for your assistance in a similar situation. Keep the exchange as equal as possible; that is, keep up your end of the bargain so that the "exchange" is not all one way. In this kind of an arrangement, the executives involved should be consulted to obtain their permission.

When your work load has increased to the point where it becomes obvious that you are unable to handle it alone, your employer may agree to provide an assistant for you on either a part-time or a full-time basis. Part-time or temporary assistance is usually preferred if the increased work load is expected to be a temporary situation. However, if you or your executive are given added responsibilities which are expected to continue indefinitely, then you may need a full-time assistant.

In delegating tasks to an assistant, be sure that you are fair in making your assignments. Divide the dull and disagreeable jobs—don't give them all to her. Share the interesting work—don't keep it all to yourself. Keep her informed with regard to the office routine so that she will be able to function effectively when you are away.

When your increased work load involves excessive typing chores, don't overlook the possibility of using a word processing center or purchasing automatic typing equipment.

How being well organized will assure
smooth-running conferences and meetings

A secretary is expected to make arrangements for meetings and conferences which may range in number from two people (including her executive) to hundreds. The simple meeting for an hour or so between her executive and another person requires, usually, only an agreement between the two as to time and place. As the number increases, however, the arrangements become more complicated.

For a meeting to be held outside your own office or conference room, the first things to be determined are where and when. If the date has been fixed, then the place must be reserved to accommodate the date; in some cases, there will be some flexibility in date so that you can work around prior reservations to obtain the space you prefer.

If you arrange meetings for your executive on a regular basis, develop your own list of available space for various types of meetings. Information in your list may include size of the space (number of people to be accommodated), seating arrangements (conference table or lecture hall), equipment available (P.A. system, slide or overhead projector, etc.), location (proximity to your office or convenience to the majority of attendees), rental costs (if any) and food service available (may range from a simple coffee break to a full-course dinner). You should also have a general idea of how much advance notice is required to reserve any of the places on your list. You may find that the advance notice required may range from a few days to several years.

More than one notice of a meeting may be necessary. A first notice may include the date and place of the meeting, the title of, or reason for, the meeting, and a list of invitees. The second notice may include a copy of the program or agenda and a card or form to be returned with a registration fee and/or a request for hotel reservations by a certain date. A third notice may be a reminder of the date of the meeting and a request that if an invitee has not already returned the registration card he should do so before the deadline. A list of those expected to attend is usually prepared and distributed in advance of the meeting, not later than just before the meeting convenes.

Although the major decisions concerning the meeting are your executive's, your responsibilities may range from routine secretarial duties to those of conference coordinator. Surely you will type the meeting notices and other printed material, whether they are reproduced in your office or printed within or outside your company. You may be expected to arrange the food service necessary, perhaps select the menus. If so, discuss your needs well in advance with the restaurant manager or a catering service and try to plan ahead for unpleasant surprises; for example, an overwhelming acceptance which doubles the number you anticipated. Even more unpleasant is an *under*whelming acceptance, particularly if the number accepting is less than the minimum number you used in negotiating for the food service. If possible, have alternative arrangements for either surprise.

You may have the responsibility of arranging overnight accommodations for out-of-town attendees. If so, you will want to negotiate well in advance with a suitable hotel or motel for the number of rooms you expect to need. You may be able to reduce the total cost of the conference, to both your company and the invitees, by cutting a "package deal" with one organization, combining the meeting place, the overnight accommodations, and the food service. If this is not possible, house the attendees at a place reasonably convenient to the meeting place.

How to use the time you save by being well organized

Assume that you are so well organized that you need never worry about achieving your goals for the day, the week, or the year. There is spare time at intervals in your work period during the year, some of which you feel free to spend in an enjoyable vacation without expecting to come back to find the office in utter chaos. What do you do with the spare moments you have earned by your efficiency?

Look for more ways to increase your efficiency. Check your files—are some of your folders becoming too thick? Review them to see if some of the papers can be destroyed, others retired to storage, and still others divided into separate folders for more efficient reference. If any group of files can be consolidated into a report, set up and prepare the report, retaining it in your office and transferring the backup material to storage.

Check the forms you are using. Are they at maximum

efficiency, or can they be improved? Care should be taken to revise forms in current use, if possible, only when the supply on hand is almost exhausted. Check to see if you could use additional forms to decrease your work load. If so, design them.

Check your job manual. Is it completely up to date? If you are advancing in your career, your job description should be constantly changing and should require periodic revision. Remember that your properly prepared job manual can be an effective argument for a promotion to a more challenging job. The job manual is also invaluable to the secretary who substitutes for you when you are away from the office, or replaces you when you are promoted to a higher position.

Check and update telephone lists, addresses, distribution lists, file index, etc. Review your reference books and order replacement copies for those which are out of date.

Be alert for opportunities to take on more responsibility. Offer to try your hand at compiling information for your executive which he usually does himself. He may be pleasantly surprised that you are not only willing but able to relieve him of more and more administrative detail.

Make every effort to work to full capacity every day. It's "job security" to come to work every morning with a full day's schedule.

Chapter 8

EFFICIENT WORK METHODS TO SAVE TIME AND MONEY

A SECRETARY HAS AN EXCELLENT OPPOR-TUNITY TO PROVE HER WORTH to her executive by saving time and money for the company. Working "hard" is not the answer. You can work "hard" all day, but what really counts is productivity—what have you accomplished? In this chapter, we will examine ways in which you may be able to increase your productivity by working, not harder, but more efficiently.

Be alert for a better way to do something to save time or money or both. Don't hesitate to copy an idea from someone else, within or outside your office, or to accept an idea or suggestion for more efficient operation. Examine the idea thoroughly before you reject it to be sure it cannot somehow be adapted to your use. Encourage and anticipate—don't resist—change. Today's best method may be outmoded tomorrow, and if you recognize and accept this, you'll never grow old mentally in the business world.

Saving money is not accomplished by pinching pennies; it is achieved by spending wisely and eliminating waste. A good secretary is always alert to possibilities for cutting costs in the operation of her office. In the following sections you will find some ideas which may suggest others more directly applicable to your own office.

How to budget time and money

A budget is very useful in many areas. We know how essential it is in planning expenditures over a period of time, and we know it is necessary in planning for consumption of materials and supplies. It is equally useful in planning the way you will spend your time.

The first step in developing a money budget is to keep a record of actual expenditures, how much and for what, for at least a month. In developing a budget for your personal expenses, for example, once you have determined how much money you have spent in a month and on what, you can estimate how much you are likely to spend in the following month on such items as rent, food, clothing, laundry and cleaning, etc.

You can develop a money budget for your office—but first, you must develop a time budget to determine how you are spending your day. Then you will know how much each facet of your job is costing the company. Very seldom will any two secretarial positions be identical; therefore, it would be impossible to set up a work analysis sheet which would be suitable for all secretaries. Figure 10 illustrates a chart which you can adapt to your own particular situation.

First develop your own code for the duties you perform in the office. Use simple abbreviations so you won't have to stop and think about the proper code (that takes time, too). Then set up a heading on a lined sheet of paper and take it from there. One day of recording your office routine may be adequate to point up areas for improvement, but since no two days are alike in the office, the more days you can record, the more accurate

Code	From	To	Minutes	Notes
P	8:30	8:45	15	Coffee
OH	8:45	9:00	15	
IC	9:00	9:05	5	Roberts contract
D	9:05	9:40	35	
V	9:40	9:45	5	Gregory-Finance

Code	From	To	Minutes	Notes
OC	4:10	4:15	5	Arnold-Chi. Off.
E	4:15	4:30	15	Deliau sales report
F	4:30	4:45	15	
OH	4:45	5:00	15	

Possible codes:

IC	Incoming telephone calls
OC	Outgoing telephone calls
V	Visitor
T	Typing
D	Dictation
E	Errands
P	Coffee, powder room
OH	Office housekeeping
IM	Incoming mail
OM	Outgoing mail
F	Filing
B	Executive
CM	Copy machine

Summary of day's activity:

IC	40
OC	20
V	30
T	150
D	60
E	15
P	30
OH	30
IM	40
OM	20
F	15
B	20
CM	15
Total	480

Figure 10. WORK ANALYSIS CHART.

will be your time estimates for the future. A work analysis sheet can be most helpful if consideration is being given to looking for additional help in the office, either through someone from the typing pool on a temporary basis or hiring a full-time assistant when your work load has been extremely heavy over a period of time.

You will have no problem figuring the time spent on each activity. The sample chart given assumes an 8-hour work day, or 480 minutes on the job. The actual cost to the company is computed on an hourly basis for the time you are *on the job*. This means that, although there are 2080 working hours a year at 40 hours each week for 52 weeks, you must deduct the time paid for but not worked, such as holidays, vacations, sick and/or personal leave, etc. Then divide your annual salary by the number of hours you are required to work during the year. Your hourly rate will be higher than the rate obtained by dividing your weekly salary by 40 hours. In the example given, an hourly rate of $3.00 can be used to make the cost per minute equal $.05. The actual cost is not so important as the proportional cost; that is, if your rate per hour is complicated to compute at cents per minute, round it off to the nearest figure easily divisible by 60: $3.10 per hour can be estimated at $3.00, $3.40 at $3.60, etc.

As it is with money, you must spend a little time in the beginning to save a lot of time later on. Developing a time budget will cost you in time; you will need to record meticulously and without fail the time you spend each day on each task. The end results will be worth much more than the time it takes to discover just how you *do* spend your work day, week, or month. To be able to estimate with a reasonable degree of accuracy the approximate time you will finish a given task, you need to know that an average eight-hour work day is spent, for example, in this way: Coffee breaks, 2 @ 15 min. ea., 30 min.; opening and working incoming mail, twice a day, @ 30 min. ea., one hour; telephone, incoming and outgoing calls, total one hour; dictation, one hour; transcription and other typing, three hours; receptionist duties (visitors), 30 min.; filing, 15 min. The rest of the day is spent in preparing to begin work and to close the office in the evening, locking and unlocking files and desk, etc.

Once you have a record of the way you spend your work day, you are prepared to review each item and compare notes to determine where you are spending too much time and where you are running short (not enough time to complete a given task). Honestly examine every facet of your work, and make a list of the ways you can cut the time required as indicated by your record of time spent.

Some of the questions you may ask yourself are these:

1. Am I spending too much time on the telephone? A telephone conversation should be as brief as possible—just long enough to accomplish its purpose without being abrupt or discourteous.

2. Is my actual filing time streamlined as much as possible? A great stack of paper can be filed in 15 minutes a day.

3. Is my typing productivity all that it should be? Check your typing and transcription speed and accuracy. There may be room for improvement in either or both.

4. Do I spend too much time in chit-chat with visitors to the office? If the visitor has business with you, take care of it promptly and efficiently; if not, be equally prompt and efficient in ushering him into your executive's office. Normally, you will not be expected to "entertain" him if he is early or your executive is delayed in meeting his appointment schedule.

Check to be sure you haven't taken too much personal time out of the office. Count the time you spend in the powder room first thing in the morning getting ready to begin work, and the last thing at night preparing to go home. Check the time you spend in preparing to go out to lunch and returning from lunch to the office. If you can cut these extra breaks by a few minutes a day, you will find that they add up to hours in the course of a month.

Budget your time properly and you will be able to

discharge your duties within normal working hours without excessive effort. Your goal should be to perform your work at maximum efficiency and be able to leave the office at the end of the day with enough energy to take care of your responsibilities at home.

Saving time by designing your own forms and rubber stamps

The time you spend in designing your own forms and rubber stamps is a good example of how a little time spent in the beginning can save a lot of time in the future. There are several things to consider in determining when you should design your own forms.

1. What will be the annual usage of the form under consideration? There is no magic number here. Even though the annual usage of a form may be four, as in the case of a quarterly report, you may find it worthwhile to design the format to record information by quarter the same way each time to simplify preparing an annual report.

2. Are you requesting information from several different sources to be consolidated into a single report? Even though you state specifically that you need information covering *a, b,* and *c,* you are more likely to get what you want if you send along a form to be completed and returned. A memorandum or letter written in response to your request will make it more difficult for you to extract and compile your data and may omit one or more of the specifics you need.

3. Is there presently available a form which can be used to serve your purpose? There are hundreds of forms available through office supply companies, and many more developed in individual companies. Be sure that there is none on the market or within your company that could be adapted for your use before you design your own form.

Once you have decided to design a form, make it as simple as possible, but be sure to include all the information necessary to fulfill the purpose for which it is being prepared. Leave ample space for the required information in each item. If there are blocks to be checked for a number of items, try to align the blocks so that a minimum of tab stops must be used to complete the form on a typewriter—if possible, save time for the person completing the form by permitting checking the blocks by hand.

In selecting the vertical spacing to be used, consider the type size likely to appear on the completed form. If the form is for your own use, adjust the vertical spacing to accommodate your typewriter. If other type styles or sizes are likely to be used, design the vertical spacing to fit elite type.

Instructions to be included on the form should be as brief as possible, but complete enough so that there will be no question in the mind of the one who fills it in. Forms which are complicated and cluttered with a lot of fine-print instructions are likely to be placed on the bottom in the "to-do" box.

A good idea in designing a form that is expected to be used indefinitely is to design a temporary form at first and give it a trial run for a while. This will give you an opportunity to detect any flaws and to revise it as necessary before deciding upon a permanent form.

Be sure to provide adequate margins so that the form can be bound or put into a loose-leaf folder. If you draft the form to be set up by a printer, be sure to check at least three things before you approve the plate: Check the alignment of any blocks for tab stops, check the vertical spacing to be sure it will accommodate an average typewriter, and check for reduction in size of print. If blocks are to be checked on a typewriter, line them up like this:

x

x

x

x

Vertical spacing should accommodate elite type, in increments of single spacing:

_____
_____

_____

_____

and so on. When the print size is reduced to get all information on one side of a sheet of paper the desired size, be sure the information can be read without a magnifying glass.

Before you decide to develop your own form, revise an existing one, or reorder, review the following checklist. (In terms of cost, it's cheaper to reorder, more costly to revise, and still more costly to design a new one.)

1. Its need and consolidation with other forms in department.
2. Need for each item (each item eliminated reduces clerical work).
3. Reduction of copy distribution.
4. Check blocks to eliminate typing.
5. Items grouped in proper sequence to facilitate recording and completion.
6. Numbering, perforation, punching, rounding corners (results in increased costs).
7. Correct column spacing for information to be entered (show number digits).
8. Margins for gripper, binding and punching.

At one time I worked for a man who was responsible for arranging a series of special lectures at the Laboratory. Once he had scheduled the speaker, he relied upon me to help with the details. Our objective was to assure a visit that would be equally rewarding to the speaker and to the Laboratory staff. Before the first speaker was scheduled, I realized that I would need a checklist to remind me of the many details I should check in advance, during, and after the lecture. Figure 11 is a form I designed as a work sheet, and it worked so well I saw no need to change it for the duration of the series. (See page 120.)

We have our own Travel Office at the Laboratory, and with so many of our people traveling throughout this country and abroad, Figure 12 is a form used in the Travel Office to expedite processing a travel request. (See page 121.)

In determining whether or not to design your own rubber stamp, first be sure that there is no standard stamp available that will suit your purpose. If not, design your own, and try to keep it as small as possible. Examples of routine rubber stamps you will want to have in your office which are not standard include your own in-plant office return address, your executive's in-plant office return address, and perhaps his full company address for use with material going outside the company.

You will want to design your own "received" stamp. You may want one as simple as this:

Date: _____

ABC: _____

File: _____

which provides space for a date stamp and your initials, a place for your executive (ABC) to initial, and the file where it is to be placed when necessary action has been completed.

A more elaborate "received" stamp may be an au-

Name _____ Lecture Date: _____

Institution: _____ Place: _____

Address: _____ Time: _____

Lecture Title: _____

_____

Special Equipment Required: _____

Publicity: Bio. Sketch: _____

               Photograph: _____

               To News Office: _____

Travel Arrival: _____

               Departure: _____

Hotel Reservations: _____

Request for Payment: _____

Expense Account Forms: _____

Security Pass: _____

Luncheon: _____

ORNL Schedule: _____

_____

_____

Figure 11. Sample checklist for arrangements for out-of-town visitors to the office.

120

RESERVATION WORK SHEET

Travelers Checks _____

Name _____ Plant Phone _____ Fee _____

Official _____ Other _____ Home Telephone _____ Fare _____

Date and Time Requested _____ Requested By _____ Cash Advance _____

Tickets and/or Cash will be: _____ Picked Up _____ Delivered ____ Bldg. No. _____ Total _____

LOCAL TRANSPORTATION SERVICE

DATE	TIME	MODE OF TRANSPORTATION	FROM	TO	LOGGED

ITINERARY

DATE	STATION	AIRLINE OR RAILROAD	FLIGHT OR TRAIN NO.	TIME	DATE CONFIRMED
LV AR					
LV AR					
LV AR					
LV AR					
LV AR					
LV AR					
LV AR					
LV AR					
LV AR					
LV AR					

HOTEL RESERVATIONS REQUESTED

HOTEL _____ CITY _____ DATES _____
PHONE NO. _____ CONTACTED _____ STATUS _____

HOTEL _____ CITY _____ DATES _____
PHONE NO. _____ CONTACTED _____ STATUS _____

HOTEL _____ CITY _____ DATES _____
PHONE NO. _____ CONTACTED _____ STATUS _____

HOTEL _____ CITY _____ DATES _____
PHONE NO. _____ CONTACTED _____ STATUS _____

REMARKS

FARE CONSTRUCTION:

Figure 12. Sample reservation work sheet for the executive's travel.

tomatic date and time stamp with additional names to facilitate routing by you or by the executive. A rubber stamp with a number of names on it, however, may be too large for efficiency—for example, a stamp any larger than 2″ x 3″ may require stamping over some of the written material on the page. You may want to simply add a blank line on the stamp suggested in the foregoing example like this:

Date: _____

ABC: _____

_____

File: _____

then on the blank line any suitable notation can be made, such as "Miller, pls. handle," "cy Hamby," or "Stone, see me."

When you find yourself writing the same names over and over on a standard "buck slip," you may want to develop your own buck slip and have a supply printed for use in your office. For maximum effectiveness, the buck slip should contain a limited number of names; it will rarely be necessary to include the name of every person in the department or every official in the company.

You may want to design a stamp for your own convenience in keeping track of the status of paper flowing through your office to other parts of the company. For example, if incoming letters addressed to your executive are frequently forwarded to someone else on his staff for action, you may want to design a stamp to provide the following checklist to be stamped on a duplicate copy of each letter forwarded (assuming that you have a stamp similar to the foregoing examples showing to whom and when the paper was sent):

_____ **Reply for my signature**

_____ **Provide information**

_____ **Reply w/cy to me**

How to time-and-motion study your office for greater efficiency

Maybe all you know about efficiency experts are jokes—if so, you should collect and read some material written about time-and-motion studies. Efficiency is essential in production work, where the cost of each item produced is directly related to the profit margin. Efficiency in your office is just as related to the profit margin, only perhaps not so easily pinpointed. The work must flow naturally with the least amount of effort and the maximum accomplishment in the shortest time.

Study your own office layout with emphasis on the flow of work. Begin with the office furniture. For this example we will assume an office in a small company with basic furniture in your office: This includes a desk, chairs for visitors, filing and stationery cabinets, and a copy machine. You may be constrained by the physical possibilities for arranging your furniture (e.g., right- or left-hand typewriter drop, placement of windows or doors), but you should try to achieve the following:

1. Your desk should face the outside door so that you will immediately know when someone has entered your office.

2. Your desk should also face the door to your executive's office for the same reason.

3. Extra chairs should be near the outside door, and preferably placed so that visitors can neither overhear conversations in your executive's office nor read any papers on your desk or in your typewriter.

4. File cabinets should be as close to your desk as possible, with the supply cabinet farther away—you should file or retrieve office papers more often than you need to replenish your stationery supplies.

5. Placement of the copy machine can also be in a remote corner. Except in a crisis, copy work should be saved so that a number of copies can be run consecutively; this saves your time, and wear and tear on the machine.

The suggestions given before in this section deal with placement of office furniture. Now let's look at each item of furniture with regard to its efficiency.

Your desk should be arranged so that it is most convenient for you because it is your principal work space. If you have an in-box for incoming outside or in-plant mail, label it conspicuously so that anyone delivering mail to your office will have no need to interrupt your work to ask which is the "in" box; the same is true for an "out" box, and each should be as convenient as possible for the person who delivers and picks up your mail.

Assuming that you are right-handed, you may prefer your typewriter on a right-hand drop, the telephone on the right side of your desk, waste basket on the right, etc. The opposite may be true if you are left-handed. In either case, you will want to motion-study your desk to be sure your work flow assures minimum effort and maximum efficiency. For example, have pencil and paper readily available to make notes any time the telephone rings or your executive or a visitor comes into the office. Organize your stationery so that your motions are kept to a minimum when you are assembling letterhead, second sheets, and carbon copies.

When you are collating material of several pages (up to five or six sheets, for example), organize your work in this manner:

Page 1, 2, 3, 4, 5, 6, staple, stack
————————————————————▶

or in the reverse order. The idea is to move across the desk in one direction. Lost motion, and lost efficiency, occur in this pattern:

Page 1, 2, 3, 4, 5, 6.
————————————————▶
Staple ◀——▶ Stack

To avoid a mad scramble for small items in your desk drawer which are not kept in the compartments provided, tape little boxes to the bottom of the drawer, close together, and have ready access to staples, keys, typing-correction materials, postage stamps, small change, etc. Use a stamp rack placed close to your stamp pad for your most-used rubber stamps.

Label each drawer in your filing cabinets to indicate the contents, and make a new label anytime you revise, expand, or contract your files so that the old label is no longer correct. This will be especially helpful if anyone other than you will need to look for something in your files—your executive, for example, or your replacement when you are away from the office. Spend seconds to type a new label and save minutes to hours of frustration for someone else who has to guess where the information may be since it isn't where the file label says it should be.

Labeling is even more important for your supply cabinet. Don't waste time trying to guess where to hunt for the supplies you need. Unless your cabinet is wide open to dust and heat, remove the tops from boxes and the wrapping from stationery so that you can readily tell which is letterhead bond or onionskin and which is plain. Label any covered box which is not plainly labeled by the supplier to indicate its contents. For example, a label reading "Reorder No. 123765" may not indicate to you or anyone else except the supplier that the box contains colored second sheets used for chron file copies.

Arrange the supply cabinet for your convenience; put materials used most often in the most accessible shelves, usually in the center, and materials required less often in the top or bottom shelves. Your individual height will determine which shelves are most convenient for you. Stretch or stoop only when necessary. The exercise may be good for you, but it's wasted motion in the office.

Weigh the advantages of a long telephone cord. The standard cord restricts your movement to about the length of your desk. With an extra few feet of cord, however, you may be able to move to your executive's door or get a paper from your file cabinet without leaving the telephone. This saves your time (carefully placing the telephone on your desk, checking to see whether your executive is available or the paper you want is in the file, then picking up the phone again—"Are you still there? I'm sorry to keep you waiting, but . . .") and keeps your caller happy: He doesn't have to listen to background noises and wonder what you are doing for so long. A few seconds of "doing nothing" but holding a telephone and waiting for a sign of life can seem aeons to a busy person.

Don't overlook little ways to save your time and avoid frustration. For example, don't wonder which is the key to the file cabinet, the desk, the credenza, etc.; label each key with a tag so that you know immediately which key fits which lock. This will help another person with authorized access to information in your office in your absence to act more effectively. The little ways you invent to save time and money will help assure you that your vacation will not be interrupted by a desperation call from the office to remind you that your life of leisure is only temporary.

The proper way to throw away paper

A very essential part of your secretarial duties is to throw away paper, and there is opportunity to save time and money in performing even this simple task. You are called upon to dispose of certain papers in the file which need be retained no longer, to replace superseded forms and imprinted stationery, to throw away such material as bulk mailing, drafts which have been completed in final form, and duplicate copies of letters or reports which are no longer needed.

In another section of this chapter you will find suggestions about ways to reuse discarded paper or to recycle it. Here we are concerned only with how to throw paper into the wastebasket.

Unless the paper to be destroyed is sensitive, that is, contains information which would be detrimental to the best interests of your office if read by the wrong person, there is no need to shred the material. If the paper *does* contain sensitive information, shred it, including all the office supplies used to prepare it, such as carbon paper, carbon ribbon, and shorthand notes.

For routine papers to be discarded, simply fold then in half and drop them into the wastebasket. Don't waste time and effort by wadding them into a crumpled ball—avoid having to retrieve a crumpled carbon copy of a letter and carefully iron out the wrinkles because you find that you really do need it after all. Avoid shredding the wrong piece of paper which contains your only record of an important name and address.

There are many motions involved in crumpling paper or shredding; there are only two in the proper way to throw away paper: (1) Fold, (2) toss. Check this for yourself and see how many motions are wasted when you needlessly crumple or shred paper.

How and when to use telecommunications

It's a great comfort to know that, when your executive is away from the office, he's as "close as the nearest telephone," and that includes any place from another office in your organization to a foreign country—unless of course he's camping out in a forest on a moose hunt. Telecommunications are also great when you need to give or receive information immediately, and even the most efficient postal service is inadequate. There is a tendency, however, to waste time and money by using one of these methods when all that is really required is ordinary mail service.

Compare the cost of a telegram in any of its various forms (telex, cablegram, etc.) with the cost of a first-class letter; do the same with a long-distance telephone call. If your transaction costs the company dollars rather than pennies, be sure the difference in cost is justified. A message by telegram provides a written record for both sender and receiver; however, an important telephone call should be confirmed in writing for the record, and that calls for the expense of additional time and money.

Time and money can be saved by substituting a note, memo, or letter for a local telephone call. Here again, if the message must be transmitted immediately ("Can your manager come to Mr. Smith's office in about 30 minutes?") a telephone response is necessary. However, if you are asked to "let us know if your executive can attend the conference two weeks from Tuesday," then a note on a buck slip may be the most efficient reply. Compare the time spent in this example, depending upon the method selected for reply: Write or type a note, "Mr. X will attend the ABC conference on 10/25,) and address an envelope; the time required to complete the job will be less, of course, if you can use an in-plant envelope rather than typing and stamping an envelope to be delivered outside the plant.

Then telephone your reply. If your call goes through immediately, fine! But time can be wasted if you run into any of these situations: (1) you get a busy signal several times before you finally reach the number. (2) you reach the number, but the person you want is on another line, and you are asked to "hold a moment" which may stretch into three or four. (3) you reach the number but the person you want is out and will call back; the "call back" happens when you are out, and you get a telephone message "returned your call." This can develop into a comedy, except that you may be surprised to learn how much it costs the company when you add up the minutes wasted on uncompleted calls, plus the value of the work you could have been doing while you were trying to save time by leaving a telephone message.

You know the importance of having frequently called numbers in a handy desk-reference gadget, but you can't possibly keep a record of all the numbers you use, especially those you use infrequently. Mark your telephone directory so that you can locate a number quickly and easily without, more than once, hunting through several pages of Johnsons or Smiths to find the right one. A highlighter pen is great to mark these infrequently called numbers.

When you have a number of phone calls to make, to set up a meeting, for example, jot down all the numbers at one time and check them off when a call is completed. It's a good idea to write down a number when you have to look it up so that you have it before you when you place the call. This will serve two purposes: If you're looking at the number as you dial, you are more likely to dial correctly and avoid the possibility of reaching a wrong number; also, you will have the number at hand in case you get a busy signal and have to call back later.

When your office has frequent written telecommunications with another office or company, keep a note of the code name as well as the telephone number of the organization.

Saving money through proper management of office supplies

Whether or not your company maintains a company stockroom to take advantage of a lower cost for quantity purchases, your responsibility as an efficient secretary is to make every item you use earn more than its cost. That is, manage the "consumption of materials" needed in your work as carefully as though it were counted in an operating statement for your office.

First let us consider that you are responsible for ordering and maintaining an adequate supply of stationery items for your office. While there is no need for an elaborate inventory system for each type of paper, form, or other office supplies you will require, you should develop a budget for each item so that you will have a good idea of how many of each you will use over a given period of time; for example, a year.

Don't be carried away by a super-salesman who extols the virtues of saving 25 percent on a double order unless you can use the double order before it rots. Remember that, when they've been around too long, paper yellows, carbon paper and typewriter ribbons lose their ink, erasers harden, ball-point pens won't work, and glue dries out—the list is endless. On the other hand, letterhead stationery and printed forms should be ordered in as large a quantity as can reasonably be used before they deteriorate or become obsolete. Your printer will usually be willing to keep on file, or return to you, the orignal plate for stationery or printed forms, and additions or corrections can be made at a cost which is nominal compared to the cost of making a new plate.

Suppose some of your stationery does become obsolete: The name or address of your company is changed, or the new president has the letterhead redesigned. Don't destroy the obsolete stationery—use the reverse side as you would plain bond for work to be drafted or have the leftovers cut into note-size paper (put into pads, if you wish). As for superseded forms which do not lend themselves to any other satisfactory use within your office, turn them over to a recycling center.

You will find many excellent opportunities for saving money through proper management of office supplies if you will look closely at postage and mailing. Check the item you are posting to be sure you are sending it in the most efficient way—this means to get the material in the hands of the addressee as inexpensively as possible but *when it is needed*. For example, for an inch-thick quarterly report which should reach the addressee at once, send it airmail and special delivery, if necessary; for routine delivery, to be reviewed at some time within the next week or so, send it as printed matter and save postage.

For overseas mail, substitute letterhead onionskin for the original letter instead of the usual letterhead bond. First-class mail within this country requires postage by the ounce, whereas overseas mail requires postage by less than an ounce, usually a half ounce. Two pages of bond paper in a #9 envelope weigh a half ounce; four pages of onionskin in a #9 envelope weigh a half ounce.

Always use an envelope no larger than necessary to mail your material. For example, don't use a 9 x 12 envelope to mail a one-page carbon copy.

For mail delivered within the plant by an in-plant mail department, watch for these ways to save money:

1. Use route slips stapled to the paper rather than envelopes if that is permitted; avoid paper clips—they have a way of hitch-hiking with other papers.

2. Fold and staple a paper or papers (so long as the package is not too bulky) and write or type the name and plant address on the outside.

3. Use in-plant envelopes which can be re-used many times—avoid using letterhead envelopes for in-plant mail.

And if you have an in-plant mail department with a postal meter, be especially careful to mark the type of postal service desired. Imagine that you are paying the postage out of your own pocket!

Look for ways to re-use office supplies. When one side of a plain file card has served its purpose, cross out the information no longer needed, flip the card over, and use the other side. You can do the same with file folders. When a folder is no longer needed with the label as typed or glued on, flip it over and label the other side—most folders are reversible—but be sure to draw a line through the obsolete label.

Up to this point, we have been assuming that you are responsible for buying your own office supplies. Now let us look at the question of saving money if you have a company stockroom.

Withdraw supplies from the stockroom as conscientiously as though you were required to pay cash for them. Replenish your supplies as necessary, but do not over-stock. Put recently acquired stock items on the bottom of the stack so that older supplies are used first. And re-use items and dispose of obsolete items as efficiently as possible. Stationery is an expense to the company, and any way you can save money for the company on secretarial materials contributes to the company profit margin just as much as savings on production materials.

Saving time by having useful reference books in the office

Every secretary should have at her fingertips at least three reference books: A dictionary, a grammar handbook, and a secretarial handbook. Furthermore, each of these books should be late editions; grammar, word usage, spelling, and secretarial procedures are all a part of our dynamic business world, and any reference book you use which is outdated contributes to your secretarial obsolescence.

Just as there are different makes and models of automobiles, so are there different makes and models of office reference books. Your company or your executive may have a preference with regard to which reference books you use, but if not, make your own selection.

Determine for yourself whether additional reference books in your office will save time and money for the company. For example, if you frequently make travel arrangements for your executive, you will save time by having airline schedules in your own office. Be sure you understand how to read them, and be sure the schedule you have is the one currently in effect— schedules are changed frequently, so take care that you don't plan a cross-country itinerary for your executive that includes a booking on a discontinued flight.

You may find it helpful to have an atlas in your office. An atlas is a convenient reference book to determine readily the name and location of any city or township not known to you. For example, should a prospective customer in Frankfort, Kentucky, be referred to the sales manager in Louisville or Lexington?

Be realistic in determining whether or not you need a reference book in your office. If you need information from a particular book on a regular basis and often, then it will probably pay for itself in short order. On the other hand, if you need to refer to that book only occasionally, don't waste money to purchase it (they're usually expensive) and don't waste the space in your office to keep it. Your local library is a fountain of information on any conceivable subject, and the reference librarian can give you specific information on anything from the price of pigs in China to the batting average of the leading slugger in the American League—and the information is usually the latest available.

Reference books are not a part of the decor of the office—indeed it may look impressive to have a Webster's New World Dictionary, Roget's Thesaurus, a Harbrace Handbook, and a Doris and Miller lined up on your desk—but they should not remain virgin territory. Keep them readily at hand, and be sure you use them!

Chapter 9

COMPOSING LETTERS THAT WILL SAVE CORRESPONDENCE TIME FOR YOUR EXECUTIVE

A SECRETARY IS MOST VALUABLE TO HER EXECUTIVE in the area of correspondence. By supplying needed information to help him write those letters he must compose himself, she saves minutes of his time. If she can prepare letters in final form for his signature on her own initiative, she can save him hours.

How to compose a letter your executive will be happy to sign

This you can't do the first day you go to work for a new executive, but after a time, when you learn his method of expression, you should be able to type a letter for his signature which he will swear (two months later) that he dictated himself. Your "composition" of a letter at first may be simply putting together some form sentences with a little variation or a personalized beginning and ending. Later, you will find that you can compose a letter from "scratch," without referring to your forms.

Remember that your principal task is to relieve your

executive of routine duties. A letter comes into the office, "Can you attend a meeting. . . .?" "Will you speak to the XYZ Club. . . .?" Type two letters for each request, one positive and one negative, and let your executive sign as he wishes. "Thank you for your invitation. . ." in either case. Then "I'll be glad to address your (group) on the subject. . . ." or "I regret that I am unable to be with you on May 19 . . ." Unless your executive knows the correspondent personally (and wants to say something like "Dear Solly, I can't make it", he will sign one or the other, and he considers the matter only once.

Of course, when you compose a letter for your executive's signature, you will be sure that the typing, the grammar, and the response are all a reflection of your excellent secretaryship. As you know, a proper impression is created by the quality of the simple mechanics of typing, but much more important is the message. Is it clear, concise, and grammatically correct? Are all necessary points covered, are all necessary questions asked (or answered)? Will your letter start a "pen pal" arrangement, generating additional correspondence to resolve the points in question?

If the letter requests information for your executive, be sure that you are asking the necessary questions so that one reply will give you the facts you need. If you are replying to a request for information, review the request to be sure that you have furnished sufficient detail so that the customer/client will have no need to write again for clarification.

Example (your inquiry): Please send me information on your 21" TV sets." Or this: "Please send me information on your Model TV67-089B, color, multi-channel TV set. I am interested in comparing prices on the console in mahogany or formica as opposed to a portable in a plastic case." Specific questions lead to specific answers.

Example: Your office receives a request for information on galvanized pipe. Your reply: "We have galvanized pipe in all sizes, lengths, and prices. We will be very happy to supply your needs." *Better:* "Our price list for galvanized pipe is enclosed. Please let us know your needs and we will be glad to ship the pipe within 24 hours after receipt of your order."

Letters you may be able to compose for your executive's signature include a congratulatory note to the new president of a corporation who is also a customer/client, or any other promotion or appointment of note, or a sincere acknowledgment of thanks to anyone who has made a special effort in your behalf to expedite an order, resolve a problem, or perform any service which can be construed as "beyond the call of duty." There are many collections of sample letters which cover every conceivable kind of situation calling for a business letter.

A business letter should be clear, concise, and correct; but it must also have the proper tone. Figure 13 is a checklist which may help in composing letters on your own initiative.

The beginning of a letter is important to get the reader's attention until he gets to the message. The ending is equally important, because that should indicate whether or not any action is expected from the reader. If you want a response, either by letter or telephone, say so at the end of the letter even though you may have included that in the message—"Please telephone my secretary at 985-2000 and let her know if we may expect you on Tuesday." If you end your letter with a question, make it positive rather than negative, and avoid alternatives. "Will you let us know by the 15th?"

When you get to know your executive, you will learn the type of correspondence he will prefer to review in draft form, and which you may prepare in final form for his signature. Prepare in draft form any information you are not absolutely certain of, and leave a blank space or indicate by a question mark the points you're in doubt about.

A message like this one could be prepared in final form: "I am pleased to enclose a brochure describing our X program. When you have reviewed this information, I will be glad to answer any specific questions you may have regarding your own interests."

Do	Avoid
Be courteous	Accusations, sarcasm, curtness, unflattering implications, anger
Be sincere	Effusiveness, exaggeration, undue familiarity or humility, flattery, condescension, preachiness, bragging
Be pleasant	Negative, unhappy, or unpleasant words
Be reader-oriented	"I" and "me" and "we want"
Be clear, direct, natural	Indefiniteness, abstract language, general statements, technical jargon
Be specific	Leaving the reader in doubt, implying alternatives if there are none
Be concise	Deadwood phrases, triteness, pomposity, archaic words, "governmentese"
Be forceful	Passive voice, "it" with no antecedent
Be well organized	Repetition, omissions
Be correct	Errors in fact, numbers, dates, choice of words
Be complete	"Half-vast" job

Figure 13. Effective letters: what to do and what to avoid.

How and when to use form letters and paragraphs

Form sentences, paragraphs, and letters can be used in reply to any routine letter from an individual or a company unknown to your executive. "The brochure you requested on our concrete pipe is enclosed. We will be glad to give immediate attention to your order when you have determined your needs." Before you adopt a form to use in your correspondence, whether it be a sentence or an entire letter, be sure it is clear, concise, and correct—be equally sure it is neither archaic nor unnecessary.

"Your letter of May 5 has been received" tells the reader nothing except that the postal service is working. "Thank you for your inquiry of May 5 about our Product X" is better. In reply to an inquiry concerning an order for merchandise which has not yet been delivered, you will want to identify the order by number and description, whether it has been sent and if so how and when. "Your Order No. 68705 for 25 boxes of Product X was shipped air freight on January 22."

The primary purpose of correspondence is communication, and although a well-written personal letter is very much a part of our business scene, quite often a form letter will communicate just as effectively as a personal note, and much faster. Figure 14 is an example of a group of form sentences and paragraphs which have been combined in a form letter. This letter was in response to my inquiry about my check which I had sent in for renewal of my subscription. The immediate reply, as well as warning that I could expect more bills until the computer caught up with my payment, was much more effective than a personal letter, dated three weeks later, would have been.

May 16, 1978

Y. Lovely
144 Pembroke Rd
Oak Ridge, TN   37830

Dear Subscriber:

Thank you for writing about your subscription.

_____ Your subscription record is in good order. The first copy sent _____.

_____ The issue(s) you missed are out of print. We have extended your subscription for the missed issues.

_____ Your subscription renewal has been received. The renewal notice which you received was prepared prior to our receipt of your order.

_____ Your order was not recognized as a renewal but was processed as a new order. Adjustment will be made with the _____ issue. You will not be charged for the duplicate copies you received. Full service will be given on your renewal order.

____X____ We have received your payment. The invoice you received was prepared prior to the receipt of your payment.

_____ Please allow 30 days for invoices to stop. Your subscription is being canceled with the _____ issue.

_____ Your subscription was canceled for non payment. We resumed service with the _____ issue.

_____ Address change requested has been made.

Sincerely,

Subscriber Service Department

Figure 14. SAMPLE FORM LETTER.

How and when to develop your own form letters and paragraphs

Your executive, whoever he is, will have his own way of expressing himself. You will soon learn whether he prefers "My dear" and "Respectfully yours" or "Jim" and "cordially" or somewhere in between. You will soon be able to identify certain phrases, sentences, and even whole paragraphs so that you can put together a "yes" letter or a "no" letter for his signature almost exactly the way he would have dictated it. For example, one executive might prefer "we would be pleased," while another would write "I shall be glad to . . ." Still another, usually military or government, will insist upon "It is necessary to inform you . . ." or "it has been determined that . . ." If you are engaged in personnel matters, receipt of an application may be acknowledged, even though an honest answer would be "no interest here, look elsewhere," with a promise to "keep your application in our active file."

Watch for your executive's favorite ways of expressing himself and type out little notes to put in appropriate spots for use in subsequent correspondence. You will then be able to select sentences, paragraphs, or perhaps even entire letters so that you may prepare replies to routine correspondence which he will be happy to sign without further consideration.

Remember always that any details you can handle yourself will save your executive for the creative thinking he is paid for.

How to avoid creating unnecessary paper work

One of the decision-making responsibilities of an executive secretary is when to generate paper and when to avoid it. The normal business letter or memorandum is expensive; therefore, any correspondence that can be eliminated should be. If the end result can be accomplished by a telephone call, don't write a memorandum.

In many cases, however, a written record is desirable, particularly in matters where there may possibly be a legal or financial question involved. "Enclosed is the financial statement you requested in your note of April 25, which is furnished before the deadline of May 5." On the other hand, a telephone call may well suffice as a reply to "please let me have your comments by November 12," if your executive has no comments to make.

When your executive initiates a piece of paper, make it as easy as possible for the person to whom it is directed to respond without creating unnecessary paper work. "We need this information; if you prefer, please telephone my office . . ." Unless your office requires the information in writing for the benefit of auditors ("Please furnish this office with a written statement of the outside selling expense for the quarter ending June 30"), then a telephone call is adequate. Learn to differentiate between the type of correspondence which is generating or perpetrating paper work and the type which is necessary for record purposes.

Another way to decrease paper work is to send out an inquiry in duplicate with a request that the reply be put at the bottom of the page and one copy returned—in this case, both your office and the addressee will have a copy for the record.

When and how to type an office memorandum

Assume that you have a piece of information which is needed by a number of offices (say five or six) within your organization. It's much more efficient to type a two-line memorandum with five copies than it is to make six phone calls, at least half of which will have to be returned because the caller is out at the moment. This assumes that the information need not be collected within the next 30 minutes. "Please let my office know within ten days if you plan to attend the symposium on July 15."

Unnecessary: "Enclosed is the corrected copy of a report which you sent to us for review on March 1," unless the report is subject to audit and you must have proof of submission. Rather than type a formal memorandum, quite often a buck slip or memo half-sheet, either of which may be hand written or rubber stamped, will be adequate.

The memorandum, however informal (and it may even be to Joe from Henry, with no last names if there is no question of who is the sender and who is the recipient), must include at least the following information: To whom, from whom, the date, the distribution of copies, if any, and initials to identify the dictator and the typist. A subject line is just as helpful on a memo as it is on a letter, and for the same reasons. A memo usually has no salutation and no complimentary close, although either or both can be included if desired. A memo may or may not be signed, depending upon the wish of the dictator. Names of individuals can be used in the "to" and "from" portions, or names of departments.

Secretaries who prepare memoranda on their own initiative may sign them instead of preparing them for the executive's signature; if this is permissible in your company, do it that way. If it isn't, but you want credit for having composed the memo, discuss the matter with your executive. He may agree to let you put your name on the memo (or even a letter going outside the company, for that matter) in some way to indicate that you are indeed the author of the correspondence. Suppose you are Sadie Marie Glutz; some possibilities are to indicate your contribution in the spot used for the initials of dictator/ typist. If your boss is Henry Jones, suggest one of the following (or any suggestion of your own): HJ/SMG/sg; SadieMarieGlutz/ sg; SMGlutz/sg; or simply sg. Should your company require the signature of a department head, section chief, or whatever, in your particular office, try putting your own name in the "from" spot and asking your boss to indicate his approval something like this:

APPROVED

_____

Henry Jones
Accounting Department

Because it is less formal than a letter, the memorandum can omit some of the niceties required for a letter outside the company addressed to a customer or a client. It should, however, follow some of the same rules for a good letter: It should be clear, concise, and correct, and should be carefully worded to be sure the tone is correct. Even if you're writing to Joe in the next office requesting information, scatter a "please" and a "thank you" as necessary; don't demand or order, even if your office has the authority to do so.

One final admonition regarding the office memorandum: Any correspondence worth typing is worth your best secretarial effort. Even good old Joe in the office next door should not be exposed to typographical errors, strikeovers, misspelled words, garbled sentences, or poor grammar. Composing and typing memos can be a good training ground for composing and typing letters for your executive's signature.

Chapter 10

BUILDING A STRONG
EXECUTIVE/SECRETARY TEAM

IT HAS BEEN SAID that behind every successful man there is a woman. To paraphrase, behind every successful business man there are probably two women, and at least one of them is his secretary. The right secretary can effectively assist her executive all the way to the top; the wrong one can anchor him on the bottom. In this chapter we will review the ways an efficient secretary can assure her future by helping her executive realize his own full potential.

How to get maximum results from the management team of executive and secretary

Your executive is the person known to top management (and top management may never have known your name) and the one who is responsible for the duties which are his. Your purpose in the organization is to help him discharge those duties and to assist him in every way possible so that he will be able to accept with confidence any additional responsibilities that he may be asked to assume. With an effective "management team"

143

of executive and secretary, there is no limit to your progress together.

To be an effective team, you must work together efficiently toward the same goals, which are the goals of the organization. Working "together" implies that he will help you to perform your duties efficiently and that you will serve him to the very best of your ability. In this chapter we will concentrate principally on ways in which you can best serve him and your company.

You must complement your executive—and to progress you must pull together and in the same direction. Whatever he needs in the way of a secretary you must either be to begin with or become, once you have served your apprenticeship with him.

The executive has first priority within your office. His wish is your command, and you willingly drop whatever you are doing to attend to his wish of the moment. If he buzzes on the intercom or simply calls out for you from his office, respond quickly. If you are talking on the telephone or if there is a visitor in your office, excuse yourself gracefully and respond to your executive. If he approaches your desk while you are busily engaged in a rush job, stop what you are doing at once and give him your undivided attention. Remember that he is the one with the ultimate responsibility for determining what is to be done in his office and when.

Anticipate his wish whenever possible. Secretaryship is a personal service, and after a reasonable time of working together, you should know his routine and preferences so that you can perform certain personal services without his asking. For example, arrange to have his coffee just the way he likes it on his desk at the time he wants it—this may be as soon as he has arrived at the office, every morning at 10:00, or any time his cup is empty.

Try to keep irritations from him. He will have enough problems which are within his realm of responsibility—handle small ones if you can without bringing them to his attention except as a last resort.

Anticipate his needs for any meeting or conference he plans to attend. Accumulate information you believe he may want to have at hand at the meeting, or which he may want to review beforehand. Remind him in advance of an appointment and ask if there is any other information you should get for him.

Help him to identify business associates or unexpected callers in the office. "Mr. Cole is calling from Omaha—you will remember his visit last fall when you were discussing possible collaboration on. . . ." "Mr. Gray stopped by to see you if you have a moment. He telephoned you last week about the Styles contract."

How and when to assume authority

Authority can be assumed only when it has been delegated. If authority has been delegated to you, accept it, assume it, and use it properly. For example, your executive has delegated to you the job of obtaining sales reports from the sales offices in his district and preparing a consolidated report within ten days after the close of each month's business. He should be able to count on having your report on his desk not later than the tenth of each month. To discharge your responsibility to him, you may have to nag the sales offices more than once, insist on your own required deadlines, and work through a coffee break or two to be on time with your report. Your executive should never learn that you have had difficulty in getting information from the sales offices, trouble with the calculations, or a monstrous typing chore.

If you have authority in any matter, don't throw it around. Discharge your responsibilities with the cooperation of those involved. Each employee should be aware of the company objectives and should work toward them; but if you run into one who presents a problem, your authority should be used only to persuade, not to demand.

Your own actions and attitudes are a reflection of your executive. Remember that the manager who gets ahead is the one who has wholehearted cooperation from those who are under his supervision. In exercising your delegated authority, you have an opportunity to help your executive develop cooperation and support from the people who can help him progress to the top.

How to give respect and earn it for yourself

Much has been written about whether an executive should be "Mr. Smith" or "Tom," and whether a secretary should be "Ms. Jones" or "Sally." "Tom" and "Sally" may be preferred in an informal office where there is little contact with clients or customers, but such informality is less desirable in an office where there are a number of visitors. An executive may call his secretary "Sally" in direct address, but to those outside the company he will refer to her as "Ms. Jones." To be certain that the proper impression of a businesslike office is maintained, a secretary should always address her executive, or refer to him, as "Mr. Smith." Even one who requests that you call him by his first name can usually be persuaded that you prefer to address him more formally, even when no one else is present. He may be secretly pleased that you wish to show him this deference.

A good secretary must have a sense of humor. With the many pressures in a business office today, a little levity now and then helps to relax your tensions. Make notes of cartoons or news items that bear on your own work, your executive's favorite hobby or sport, or office situations, and be prepared to speak of them to him as appropriate. Risque comments and stories, however, have no place in the business office.

The equality of men and women which is receiving so much attention today should not be taken too literally, especially with regard to language. If your vocabulary is adequate, you can get your point across by using acceptable language without resorting to vulgarity. And no matter how much is legislated about women having equal rights with men, women are indeed different from men—and, as the French say, "Vive l' différence!" A woman can keep her femininity without losing her equality. Keep your language businesslike, your behavior above reproach, and your femininity a secret weapon.

Communicating with your executive: when to speak up and when to listen

A recognized problem in the area of management, from top to bottom, is the one of communication. You can do your part to solve this problem by assuring that there is ease of communication between you and your executive. When he speaks, you listen—when he gives instructions, details a job assignment, or dictates a report. Even more important, however, is communication when nothing so specific is involved.

An executive may use his secretary as a "sounding board" whether he realizes it or not. If you have been a management team over a period of years, he will appreciate the value of having you as a "sounding board" to talk aloud about a business problem of concern to him and the company.

He may know that no matter how long one thinks about a decision to be made, how long he "mulls it over" in his own mind, talking about it will clarify certain points to an extent which will permit reducing the situation to writing. He may feel a little idiotic striding across his office talking to himself, even though this is one way to "talk out" the problem. It's much better to have a listener, and not one who will demand equal time, such as a peer. What better listener, then, than his secretary?

When your executive wants to talk, listen to him—and listen with both ears, an open mind, and a receptive spirit. Be silent but alert, be interested but not nosy, be responsive but don't interrupt his train of thought. If necessary, take a few notes concerning comments or questions that may occur to you as he talks, but you have no opportunity to mention at the time.

When your executive asks for your opinion, give one only if you have one. If you do have an opinion or an idea, speak up! Even if what you say won't solve the problem, it may give him an idea for another approach to the situation. If you can't think of anything at the moment, say so—"May I think about that for a bit and see if I have something to suggest later?"

For example, the executive is torn between two candidates for promotion to a vacancy in his department. One has longer service with the company, almost no record of absenteeism, a reputation as a loyal company employee who deserves recognition for his devotion to duty over the years. The other is younger, has fewer years of service with the company, but is aggressive, has the knack of inspiring those who work with him, and is charged with new ideas, some of which are "way out." Your executive talks aloud to you in an effort to clarify his own thinking concerning the decision he must make. Listen, and if he asks for your comments, give him any input or feedback you can. "X is head of a section that is split, half in favor and half against his way of doing business. Y has the whole-hearted support of his group, even if what he is doing is wrong." A secretary can often supply the nuts and bolts viewpoint of the supervised which escapes the supervisor.

A secretary should speak up when she has any reason to believe her executive is acting without full knowledge of a situation or when he is in danger of transmitting incorrect information. For example, if your executive tells you to call a client and tell him that the Director of Sales in Hackensack is Joe Hudson and you know that is not correct, simply "remind" him that Joe retired at the end of last month and the present director is Bill Johnson.

Speak up at any time you have information that you believe your executive should know. If he does not know that the head of one of his departments had emergency surgery over the past weekend, if he does not know that one of his most important clients won the bowling tournament last night, if he does not know that one of his best foremen just became a proud grandfather, speak up. If he would want to know these things, you will help him by keeping him informed. He can offer congratulations or sympathy, as appropriate, and maintain the necessary personal relationship with his employees and clients.

Speak up any time you have an idea or a suggestion concerning ways to improve your office procedures, to expedite certain tasks, to eliminate obsolete forms or unnecessary paper work. Keep your executive informed of any changes in procedures or method of performing clerical tasks occasioned by changes in company policies, legislation, or governmental bureaus. He may have read the general information without relating it specifically to his own responsibilities; be sure that he realizes what any such change means to the work of your office.

How to help your executive budget his time

The ability to communicate with your executive is an invaluable asset to you both when we talk about helping the executive budget his time. A few minutes at the beginning of each day to review together his schedule of appointments, meetings, etc., will point up immediately any conflicts or problems. Your executive may be one who prefers a tight schedule, with a fixed beginning time and a fixed ending time as well for each of his appointments. On the other hand, he may prefer a loose schedule with only the beginning time fixed, taking as long as necessary to conclude the business at hand.

You will have letters and reports to prepare, incoming mail to be reviewed, telephone calls to place or to answer, and the other miscellany of the office. He will have appointments, meetings, luncheons, conferences, and visitors, all of which must be fitted into the day's schedule. If your executive prefers to dictate to you personally rather than use a dictating machine, time must be allowed for this from both your schedules. Reviewing the day's schedule in advance will help to plan for maximum accomplishment, but allowance must also be made for the unanticipated. A time budget, like any other, is made as realistic as possible according to the information at hand, but must be flexible enough to cope with the extraordinary. A time budget made up at the beginning of each day may help convert what might be chaos to an orderly and efficient day.

If an appointment or meeting is to take place in your office, you have only to be sure your own executive is present at the designated time.

Although you will have no control over the people who are expected in your office at a certain time, you can help your executive keep on his schedule. If Mr. X arrives early for an

appointment, inform your executive and let him decide whether
to see him at once or wait until the appointed time. If other
people learn that your executive is prompt in meeting his appointments, they will make a special effort to be on time also.

When your executive has an appointment outside his
own office, remind him to leave the office with ample time to
arrive at his destination at the appointed hour, whether the
meeting is next door or across town.

When and how to interrupt the executive
who is in conference

An executive may be in conference with one person or
with several. If he has allocated his time for an appointment, he
will usually prefer to conclude the business without interruption. If he is able to do this, he is better able to keep to his
planned schedule. However, there are times when he will want
to be interrupted. As his secretary, it is your business to know
when and how to interrupt.

You should know from the nature of the appointment
whether to interrupt for anything less than an emergency. You
and your executive will arrive at an understanding as to whom
and for what he can be interrupted. He may want to take a
telephone call at any time from his own supervisor or from a
member of his family; on the other hand, he may prefer to be
undisturbed unless the plant is on fire. Normally, if you can't
decide whether or not to interrupt, you can leave the decision to
the caller: "May I ask him to telephone you later?" Unless it is an
emergency, this is usually satisfactory with the person who is
calling.

If you know he wants to be interrupted, there are
several ways to do it gracefully. Remember that you are also
interrupting the other person or persons who are with your
executive, and they must not be made to feel that their business
is not important. If you have an intercom, a brief buzz (not a
prolonged blast) will suffice to get the executive's attention. Be
as brief as possible, but tell him what he needs to know: "The

manager of the Helsinki plant is on an overseas call." He will decide whether to take the call in his office or perhaps excuse himself to take the call over your telephone.

If you do not have an intercom, or the intercom is audible to other people in the room and your message is confidential, type a note, peck politely on the closed door, enter at once and hand the note to your executive. If you have an urgent message for someone else attending the meeting, type a note and deliver it in the same way. If there are several people in the room and you aren't sure which one is the person the message is for, simply say quietly "I have a message for Mr. Brown."

There are those who advocate that the secretary enter the conference room without first rapping on the door, and others who contend that she should knock and await permission to enter. You do whatever your executive prefers. The most efficient method of interrupting is to knock, enter immediately, and take care of the business at hand. In this way, the conference participants know they are to be interrupted, conversation will cease immediately, you may enter, deliver your message, and exit in a matter of seconds.

Handling personal work for your executive

Regardless of the position of your executive, there will be a certain amount of personal work you will be expected to do for him. In a small business where you work for the owner of the company, there is likely to be much more than in a large corporation where both manager and secretary have a heavy workload of company business. The personal work may consist of keeping his personal checkbook, a record of his stocks, bonds, and other investments, typing personal correspondence, filling out income tax forms, and perhaps other things as well.

If anything, the personal work you do for your executive should be treated as more confidential than company business. Never leave personal work exposed where anyone else can see it. Your executive's bank balance, investments, and other personal affairs are nobody else's business. Certainly the admonition to keep the boss's business affairs confidential applies as much if not more to his personal business—don't answer any questions about it if anyone is impolite enough to ask.

Secretaryship is a career of personal service, and the personal business must be performed willingly and just as meticulously as company business.

How to make traveling as painless as possible for your executive

Almost every executive travels to some extent; he may travel occasionally and for short distances, or he may travel extensively in this country and abroad. His secretary's job is to make traveling as painless as possible for him.

Discuss with your executive his preference with regard to travel arrangements. If you are communicating, you will soon learn whether he prefers a tight or a loose schedule, if he is averse to night flying or late hours, and which hotel he prefers in the cities where he travels most often. Encourage him to give you his business schedule and then, considering his preferences, plan the best possible itinerary for him.

You may want to keep travel schedules at your finger tips if you make travel arrangements for him regularly and often. Otherwise, develop a working relationship with your travel office (if there is one within your organization) or with your local travel bureau. Simply transmit your executive's wishes with regard to travel and let someone else worry about the tickets, limousine pick-up, rent-a-car, or what have you.

Whether you make his travel arrangements or trust them to another office, don't wait until 30 minutes before plane time to check to be sure everything is in order. Know the normal lead time required to check on his hotel accommodations, plane tickets, limousine or taxi pick-up, travel advance (if any) and all the other details to assure a smooth, orderly departure from the office.

Keep a copy of his itinerary in the office with telephone numbers where he can be reached in case of emergency; a nice gesture is to prepare a duplicate for his wife. He may want to give it to her personally or have you mail it to her, but this is another point to discuss with him; follow his instructions.

If there is pre-departure paper work, be sure it is prepared and submitted properly and sufficiently in advance so that there will be no last-minute crisis. Send him on his way prepared for his trip and unruffled by mismanaged arrangements. When he returns, be equally adept in taking care of the post-travel arrangements. He will probably have an expense report to prepare, either to submit to the company for reimbursement or to retain for his own personal income tax records. See to it that he prepares, or gives you the information to prepare for him, whatever record is necessary to assure that he claims all the income tax deductions for business expenses to which he is entitled.

He may travel abroad, which somewhat complicates the arrangements. If a passport is required, one can be obtained through your local post office, normally within about two weeks. He may need a visa, depending upon the foreign country he proposes to visit and the length of time he expects to be there. Your company travel office or your local travel bureau will be able to advise you on this matter. A visa may require as much as six weeks or longer to obtain, again, depending upon the country to be visited; be sure your application is made sufficiently in advance so that planned travel arrangements need not be postponed.

When foreign travel is involved, your local bank can be most helpful. Traveler's checks can be exchanged for local currency in most foreign countries he will be visiting, but more important than obtaining currency are such matters as "How much do I tip a porter, a waiter, a taxi driver, in francs, lire, or rupees?" Most banks are able to supply information on the equivalent value of the foreign monetary unit with relation to the American dollar as well as suggestions for tipping in the various countries (in native currency), and many travel bureaus have the same or similar information.

To help your executive travel as painlessly as possible,

whether for business or for pleasure (if you also arrange his vacation travel), encourage him to give you a general idea of where he is going, when, why, and how long he expects to stay at each stopover on his trip; make all the necessary arrangements to see that he has a well-planned, well-organized journey, and help him with the necessary follow-up paper work when he returns to the office. As his secretary, your job is to see that all he has to do is travel.

Handling the office when your executive is away

An executive may be away from the office for weeks at a time: a good secretary can keep the office on an even keel with or without him, and a good part of the time it is without him.

An absent executive eliminates from the secretary's schedule many of the pressures of a normal day. She can plan her schedule more accurately when she doesn't have to allow time for his dictation; arranging, scheduling, or canceling meetings or appointments; answering the intercom or getting his coffee.

When he is to be away, have an understanding with him before he leaves about how you should manage the office in his absence. Following are some suggestions regarding situations which may arise while he is gone.

Emergencies sometimes occur between the day the executive leaves on a trip and the time he is scheduled to return. If possible, know how to reach him by telephone at any given time (plus or minus a few hours at a time when he is en route) in case of an emergency. If you are not able to reach him by telephone or telegraph, have an understanding with him that he will telephone the office at regular intervals. Your executive may prefer to touch base with the office at least once a day (or whatever interval of time he prefers) at some time convenient to him. Keep a list of things he will want to know, questions you need to ask, and messages he will want to receive so that you will be prepared when he telephones. (Keep the list whether he telephones you or you call him.) Note that the emphasis is on information that *he* will want and that you *need* to know; don't waste time and money giving him details on matters that will wait for action until he returns to the office.

While he is away, incoming mail should be sorted into categories, which may be urgent, routine, review and toss, or whatever is appropriate for your office. Telephone calls, visitors, and matters requiring immediate action may be referred to another office in your organization. No doubt there will be many questions which you can answer in his behalf, letters and memoranda which you will be able to answer on your own, and other letters which can be held for his personal reply when he returns to the office. Depending upon when he is scheduled to return, you may want to acknowledge a letter over your signature to let the writer know that his communication has been received but that the reply from your executive will be delayed.

You may want to keep a daily log of what has gone on in the office, names of visitors, telephone calls, meetings he has missed, problems or questions which have come up and you couldn't handle. He may want to review it, but even if he doesn't, it will serve as a check list to remind you that some of the items listed, although not urgent, should be discussed with him when time permits.

With a less hectic schedule when he is away, you should have time to do some of the chores you have let accumulate because of lack of time. This is a good time to type a revised list of names and addresses for distribution lists, review the files to see if some of them can be retired, clean out desk drawers, straighten up the supply cabinet, have your typewriter or other office machines cleaned and serviced, or make up a new personal telephone directory.

Greet him upon his return to the office with neat and orderly desks (yours and his) with his accumulated mail in appropriate stacks—put "good news" urgent mail on top; he'll get to the bad news soon enough. Be prepared for a deluge of paper, what has accumulated in his absence and which he will return to you as soon as possible, as well as the stack he will very likely unload from his briefcase. The telephone will ring off the wall, visitors will be in and out of the office, he will summon you constantly, and you will soon be happily back in the normal hectic routine.

Chapter **11**

HOW TO TACTFULLY HANDLE
PROBLEM SITUATIONS
WITH THE MANAGER

NOBODY'S PERFECT. In this chapter we will consider some of the characteristics of managers that create problems for the secretary and how one might cope with them. There is no magic formula here. You will not be able to change your executive overnight; what you will need to do is to persuade him to change himself—his habits, his attitudes, and his method of operation. It won't be easy.

But before you try to figure out how to help your executive with *his* problem, make sure you're not a part of it!

Some "don't evers" about executives

As a good secretary, you know the "don't evers" about executives; however, it's good to review them occasionally to be sure you aren't slipping.

Don't ever criticize your executive, not to him and certainly not to anybody else; keep his imperfections confidential.

Don't ever violate his confidence. You may impress "the girls" by being in-the-know on matters about which rumors are flying, but if you want to keep the paycheck coming, keep your mouth shut.

Don't ever discuss your personal problems with him; he has enough of his own. From nine to five your complete attention should be devoted to the office.

Don't ever let him suspect that you are annoyed with him. He may have a bad day occasionally and he may be abrupt or downright unpleasant with you for no reason. Keep calm, and bear with him until he regains his own composure. He may never apologize, which is not necessary; but, if he does, simply smile and let him know that he's such a prince most of the time that you don't mind if he relaxes his tensions at your expense once in a while.

Don't ever lose your temper with him. Loss of temper is nearly always accompanied by loss of common sense, and if you are impertinent, he can always have the last word: "You're fired!"

Don't ever shed tears in the office. Few men can stand a weeping female, and he is probably no exception. Tears may result from loss of temper, which shouldn't happen, from hurt feelings (don't wear them on your sleeve—a secretary should have the hide of a rhinocerous), from exhaustion (a crisis-every-five-minutes day), or whatever your own hang-up is that makes you cloud up and rain all over the place. If you feel any tears coming on, run to the ladies' room. You'll need to repair your makeup anyway.

If you don't have any problems with this section, you are ready to proceed with the rest of the chapter.

How to eliminate crises created by a "crisis creator"

The "crisis creator" wakes up every morning to a brand new world—and he's always two weeks behind in his deadlines. Instead of planning and organizing, he's completely unplanned and disorganized. He frantically begins, on the day it is due, a report that normally takes a week to prepare.

He is consistently late for meetings and appointments. He has never given a thought to the fact that when *he* is late for an appointment or a meeting, he is wasting not only his own time but the time of other people as well.

Among the problems facing his secretary are these: Overtime work, coming in early in the morning, staying late in the evening, working straight through lunch, or possibly all three; telephone calls back and forth to explain that the executive will be late or that an appointment or meeting will have to be rescheduled; inability to plan her own work around his erratic schedule. If you have this problem, you may never be able to eliminate all the crises in your office, but you will be able to hold them to a minimum by training him slowly and carefully.

Since he probably has no idea on Monday what he will be doing the rest of the week, develop your own schedule for him based upon all information you have at hand, then compare your estimate with the schedule he follows. In time you should be able to guess, fairly accurately, what he will be doing at least part of the time each day. Gently remind him in advance of a meeting; phrase your reminder as a helpful question: "Will you need any material from the file for your two o'clock meeting?" "Will you want to take to the ten o'clock conference a list of those who are expected to attend?"

Carefully watch for and note deadlines on requests for information, reports, etc. Collect on your own initiative any material you can which will be of help to him, and don't hesitate to ask if you can assemble or develop additional material for him. He may not realize just how much of the "leg work" you are able to do for him.

If he accuses you of nagging, your response will depend upon your individual personalities and how well you get along together. You may admit that you're nagging because if you don't he'll miss his deadline; on the other hand, discretion may dictate that you admit only that, as a good secretary, you are just making sure that you are discharging your responsibility to remind him of his schedule.

Do everything possible to help him develop the habit

of discussing with you, the first thing every morning, his plans for the day. With a little communication, you'll soon be able to remind him on Monday morning about a report due on Wednesday or next week. If you're tactful enough, he will accept your comments pleasantly as reminders and learn to depend upon you to keep things from bogging down on his desk.

How to discourage the manager who has something on his mind besides business

One would expect the "lover boy" type to be a fledgling in the business world who has not yet learned to take his job seriously. This is not always so: A "lover boy" may be an otherwise respected business man who is in his dotage.

With this type of manager, his secretary has to have the agility of a gazelle to keep out of his reach. He is prone to pat her on her hand, her arm, or anywhere else. His ultimate goal is to have a secretary and a playmate for one paycheck. He fails to realize that the company is paying her to work 40 hours a week on company business, not monkey business. Even if hanky-panky between boss and secretary is not frowned on for moral reasons, it's frowned on by management if it's done on company time.

Whether you are afflicted with this type of obnoxious individual in your own office or he is some other secretary's executive, your general attitude and response should be the same. Be sure that your own behavior is above reproach. As an efficient secretary, you should maintain your dignity and poise under all conditions and circumstances—this is not easy with a determined and predatory male.

Make every effort to discourage personal remarks and advances at the very earliest stage. If he is your executive and persists, explain your position frankly and firmly. You are paid for your professional services as a secretary, and you are "his" from 9:00 to 5:00 for company business only. Your personal time is your own and you prefer to select your personal associates outside the company.

In an extreme case where he insists that, in order to continue working for him, it will be necessary that you meet with him in the evening or travel with him on business trips, look for another position. An executive seldom marries his secretary, and very few relationships between him and his secretary, which combine business and pleasure, endure for very long. At the worst, the latter arrangement may end up in a sordid headline, with your name in 30-point type.

How to educate the "do-it-himself" type

This type of manager does what he's paid for on a part-time basis only (engineering, production, selling, etc.)—the rest of the time he's doing secretarial work. He doesn't really know what a secretary is capable of doing, so the "girl in his office" does only the routine typing and filing.

He makes his own travel arrangements and reservations—he doesn't want his secretary to mess them up. He makes his own appointments and never tells her what they are—when a visitor shows up in the office, she has fun trying to guess who he is and what he wants.

He answers his own phone and places his own telephone calls, swearing at the long-distance operator while his secretary files her nails and watches the clock. He opens his own mail and passes it along to his secretary only when he has finished with it, keeping everything of importance on his own desk.

Every word he dictates, every mark he puts on a piece of paper, is his very own brain-child, and everything he composes he views as a literary masterpiece. Woe to his secretary if she tries to dress up his grammar, straighten up a meaningless sentence, or eliminate an unnecessary comma! He expects his secretary, who knows better and reluctantly puts her initials on the letter as typist, to continue sending out letters reading "enclosed herewith," "pursuant to your request," and "beg to advise." He expects her to type in his commas which are sprinkled at random and to ignore some of his more involved efforts that result in such beauties as "one are" and "these is."

If you have this type of a problem executive, you have an intensive training job to do before you can call yourself his secretary. The "do-it-yourself" person has probably never had a secretary, or if he did, she failed in any effort she ever made to train him properly.

Surprise this type of executive with your capabilities. With regard to travel arrangements, anticipate his needs, type up a neat schedule with alternate flights, indicate those serving meals, and suggest overnight accommodations that will be most convenient for his business appointments. Be as nosy as necessary to find out what's going on in the office. Ask him what appointments he has, with whom, and what time. He may be reluctant to tell you, but point out that you need the information so that you may properly discharge your duties.

Listen to his part of a telephone conversation if you can. You may be able to learn that he's planning a trip to New York next week or that he's expecting a visit from a prospective client on Tuesday. Let him alone if he wants to answer his own telephone and place his own local calls, but try to persuade him to let you place the long-distance calls to save his time.

Use your most persuasive ability to urge him to delegate to you the job of opening the mail. Explain the need to date-stamp the mail as it is received and the assistance you can provide in attaching back-up material as appropriate, and in sorting the mail for him with priority matters separated from the routine.

The person who wants to keep everything of importance on his own desk is next to impossible to train out of this habit. Concentrate on getting him to agree to let you open the mail, and you will at least be able to make an extra copy of everything of importance that you know will disappear the minute it hits his office. Otherwise, you will have a mad scramble through the mess on his desk when he is searching for an important paper. (He won't be able to find it, and he will accuse you of misplacing it.)

Another reason to work on getting permission to open the mail is to give you an opportunity to draft a note or two here and there in reply to incoming correspondence. He may not realize that you are capable of performing this service—and he may come to appreciate that you know your grammar well enough to help him with his when he composes his own letters.

Communication is the key to an effective management team of manager and secretary. The greatest secretary in the world to one person can be a complete failure to another—the difference is communication. Try to learn to communicate with him—comment or question him intelligently about business matters concerning his responsibilities. It may be difficult, but it isn't impossible, to convince him that you are a good secretary, not just a clerk in the office.

Enduring the autocrat

The autocratic person doesn't believe in the "management team" of executive and secretary. He simply gives the orders and she carries them out. Unless he gives her specific permission to do so, she may not order, on her own initiative, so much as a box of facial tissue.

The autocrat is a heckler. His secretary could increase her productivity by 100 percent if he'd only let her alone. He gives her a ten-page report to type and checks every five minutes to see whether it's ready. When he gives her a long letter to type "at once," he stands over the typewriter, breathing down her neck, until it's finished.

He worries her to death with instructions. He not only tells her what to do, but how, down to the last minute detail. He ignores the fact that she's human and capable of a little initiative herself—he considers her a robot and provides the programming.

The autocrat is also a hunter. His secretary would be

chained to her desk if it weren't illegal. He runs up and down the hall looking for her the minute he realizes she isn't in the office; if he can't find her, he sends another girl to get her out of the powder room. He times her lunch period and coffee breaks to the minute—he really believes in a day's work for a day's pay.

You will note that this section is headed "enduring" the autocrat. Unfortunately, a secretary is quite often unable to train this type of manager at all—even his analyst would have a problem; however, don't give up without a struggle.

For example, if you want something for the office which he has not himself ordered, extract the order from him. Let's use a new typewriter for this example. Collect and itemize the reasons why *the office* needs a new typewriter (not you, but the office, and therefore *he* needs a new typewriter). Also itemize the reasons why the old one will no longer suffice. Present your case reasonably, stand ready to defend it, and let him decide to give the order to buy a new one.

You may be able to train him out of his heckling habits. When he gives you a lengthy rush job, explain that the ten-page report will require at least two hours of typing time if you don't have too many interruptions. Suggest to him that you type better and faster if there is no one watching you. Estimate the time you'll have the task completed and promise him the finished product "by 2:00 this afternoon." And meet your deadline.

For the person who gives you detailed instructions over and over, anticipate them; and when he pauses for breath, detail them back to him to show that you understand exactly how he wants the job done. Be sure that your manner is always deferential; never be impertinent. If you manage properly, you should in time be able to head off much of the detail by simply asking if this is to be done following the format of the "X" report.

The best executive will usually prefer that his secretary be at her desk at all times to answer the telephone, greet visitors, and take care of the office routine; but he will be reasonable enough to allow her time out of the office for a coffee break, lunch, or a trip to the ladies' room. To cope with the hunter, try telling him when you leave the office where you are going and when you expect to return. "I'm going for coffee, and I'll be back at 10:15." "I have something to pick up in the mail room, but I should be back in a few minutes." "I'm going down the hall for a moment . . ." If he's occupied when you leave the office, explain in advance that when this is the case you will leave a note for him in a certain spot so that he will know at all times where you are and when you'll be back. He may be able to curtail his desire to track you down if he's reasonably assured that you haven't run away for the rest of the day.

Let us hope that he has other and better qualities that make it possible for you to endure the autocrat and be reasonably happy in your job.

How to extract information from the executive who doesn't want to tell you anything

This type of manager truly believes that he should never tell his secretary anything that is confidential because everybody knows a woman can't keep a secret. This man's secretary is the last to learn what's going on in her own office.

At his worst, he is a real clam. Not only does he refuse to discuss confidential matters with her, but he fails to recognize that she needs to know as much as possible about his own responsibilities so that she will be able to understand what she can and should do to be of maximum assistance to him in the office. He never gives a second thought to whether or not a change in policy or a change in staffing can affect her work. She must rely on information from another office, one of the other secretaries, or just plain scuttlebutt to keep abreast of company matters which are initiated outside her office.

To cope with this problem, you must first gain his confidence. Be absolutely certain that you don't "leak" information from your office. Be conservative in what you tell other people, giving only enough information to discharge your duties competently. If you hear something from a person outside your office or company that affects your executive's area of responsibility, select the proper time and way to speak of it to him. "I understand that the purchasing and receiving department is to be split into two separate departments. Will this mean that our purchase orders must be submitted with a longer lead time?" He has probably heard about the proposed change, but failed to realize that it could have a direct effect on his planning.

Exhibit your interest in the company's operations by asking pertinent questions from time to time. "Since our sales quota is to be increased, will we have to hire more salesmen?" It will take time to convince him that you are more interested in your job than you are in simply taking home a paycheck, but if you succeed in getting him to discuss his problems and his responsibilities with you, you will be able to lead him gently to the way an executive should function when he has a competent secretary.

How to get out the office work even if your executive is civic-minded

Executives are frequently active in civic affairs, and indeed many of them are encouraged by the company to participate in community activities. If the workload is sufficient to justify it, a full-time secretary may be assigned to the outside job. A more usual arrangement, however, is for the executive's company secretary to perform the additional secretarial work as a part of her regular duties.

An executive will make a statement like this: "Certainly I take an active part in community affairs. My secretary can always squeeze in a few more letters or phone calls during office hours." He may be right—if her regular workload is relatively light and if the Civic Club paper work is not too demanding. But for the secretary who is already working to capacity every day, "squeezing in" a few extra letters or phone calls can pose a problem.

As a secretary, you must remember that your job is to perform the tasks your executive assigns to you, regardless of their nature, so long as they are not illegal. You should be able to determine the proper priority of work by using your own judgment; but if you have any question, point out the problem to him and let him make the decision. "I can either finish the sales report or get out the Civic Club meeting notice this afternoon—which job can wait until tomorrow morning?"

With the proper attitude, you may find that you can enjoy a variation in the kind of secretarial work you are asked to do in connection with community activities. For instance, if you work for a doctor, much of whose correspondence and reports you can't really understand, you may develop a real interest in your local school board or the city council.

The work you do for your executive that is not directly related to the objectives of the company may assume overwhelming proportions. He may not realize that he is expecting you to do too much secretarial work that is not company business. If you are asked to type themes and school papers for his children, address invitations and Christmas cards for his wife, and mail 200 letters a month in connection with his community activities, you may discover that you can't do all that is expected of you within normal working hours. When this happens, discuss the matter with him and be prepared to suggest alternative solutions to the problem. One possibility is to offer to do his personal work after hours for additional pay; another is to suggest that he get someone else to help with the workload, either during office hours or after. Whether he or the company bears the additional expense is his decision.

Always remember that in any "discussion" with your executive, be reasonable and objective—keep emotion out of it. Don't whine or complain, simply present the facts and try to help, not hinder, his arriving at a solution satisfactory to you both.

How to nail down the disappearing executive

This person is the despair of a majority of secretaries the world over. His attitude is "I don't tell my secretary where I'm going every time I leave the office; it's none of her business." He appears and disappears at will, and when he's gone, only God knows where to find him.

If your executive has this bad habit, he must be trained out of it. First he must be trained that he is wrong, that his whereabouts is very much your business; not to satisfy your own curiosity, but so that you can do the best possible job for him.

Explain to him that he doesn't have to ask your permission to leave his own office, but that his best interests will be served if he lets you know whenever he will be away for more than a few minutes. When *his* superior calls, he doesn't want to hear from you that your executive is not in, you don't know where he is, and have no idea when he'll be back.

There could be an urgent call within the company, or from his wife, or from a business associate ready to sign a million-dollar contract. Even if he doesn't want anybody *else* to know where he is or what he's doing, suggest that he keep you informed so that you will know when and how to get an urgent message to him. Convince him that you will not give out to *anyone* any information he doesn't want disclosed (not even his wife, if he says so). For anything less than urgent, assure him that you will take care of the matter yourself or stall until he returns to the office.

Work diligently at training the disappearing executive to keep you informed of his whereabouts. It will be well worth your effort. Otherwise, you may call a dozen different offices and other organizations before you finally locate him—to give him a message that the president of the company wanted him in a meeting 30 minutes ago.

You may have an executive similar to one who once said "There are times when I don't want to be disturbed, even for a crisis—and I don't want my secretary or anybody else to know where I am." If this is the case, you can only urge him to hold his hermit sessions to a minimum and simply tell you that he will be incommunicado for the rest of the day. Then you will be fulfilling your responsibility as his secretary if you relate the message to anyone who calls: "Mr. Smith is out of the office for the rest of the day . . ." and, if necessary, "I'm sorry, he cannot be reached by telephone."

How to keep from getting ulcers if you report to more than one manager

Two problems are compounded for the secretary who serves more than one master: The whereabouts of more than one, and the priority of the work.

A secretary who must keep up with the work for a number of men has no time to telephone around the organization or run up and down the hall to find a missing person. If a manager doesn't answer his buzzer and has left no forwarding address, have it understood that he is to be content with a message in his mailbox.

Each man who shares the services of a secretary is prone to consider his work more important than that of the others and expects the secretary to agree with him: He is frequently annoyed when any of his work is delayed while another's is completed. Ask your managers to agree among themselves on the priority of the work and inform you of their decision. They probably won't do it, since none of them will be willing to agree that any of his work is of lower priority than that of any other. Therefore, you may very well be required, for survival, to develop your own order of priorities.

First, be able to tell any manager how long it will be before he can expect an item of work to be completed. And be realistic: allow time for interruption by the other managers, telephone calls, visitors, etc. Time yourself with regard to dictation by each person; take into consideration whether he dictates rapidly or slowly, whether the transcript is to be in draft or final form, whether editing by you is required and how extensively, and the length of the dictated material. Dividing your work-time among several managers, you'll have to make many such time estimates in order to plan your work schedule. When you report to more than one manager, the effective organization of your daily work is imperative.

Second, divide your work into priorities: Top, urgent,

and routine. Type out a list indicating the jobs in each category. Post the list by your desk and give each manager a copy.

Under "top" you may put telecommunications and travel arrangements for trips scheduled within the next week or so. "Urgent" matters may include first-class letters concerning company business and reports and manuscripts with early deadlines. The "routine" stack will be requests for information needed at some time in the future, routine reports and memoranda, personal correspondence for the managers, and anything else that does not have a stated or obviously early deadline.

Third, with your list include lead-time preferred for each type of job. For example, you may need three weeks for a 100-page manuscript, or ten days before planned departure for travel to be arranged. Items can be reclassified as necessary from one priority to another.

You may like one manager more than another, but whatever your preferences may be, don't play favorites. Assign priorities on a completely impersonal basis. Consider each task in the light of your primary objective: That is, doing your job promptly and properly for your office and your company.

A position as secretary to a group of individuals can be valuable training for a top secretarial job. It encourages learning many methods of survival in the highly competitive business world. The "shared" secretary must have the tact of a diplomat, the endurance of a horse, the hide of an armadillo, the patience of Job, and a drawer full of tranquilizers. If you persevere, one of your many managers may be promoted and request you for his personal secretary.

Chapter 12

MAINTAINING SATISFACTORY
OFFICE RELATIONS
WITH OTHERS

IF OTHER PEOPLE ONLY WOULD BEHAVE the way we think they should, we wouldn't have any problems; unfortunately, they don't. Getting along with other people is sometimes called "human relations." Human relations is the art of getting another person to do something for you that he doesn't want to do and then have him thank you for the privilege of serving you. As with anything else worthwhile, this is not easy.

Although there are some men who are difficult to deal with, other *women* frequently cause problems for the secretary. A good secretary knows how to trade on her femininity to win from men the cooperation or assistance she needs. What we will consider mainly in this chapter are ways to get along with other women in business. But remember that in many instances you may substitute "man" for "woman" and the ways for coping with the situation are the same.

What you will *not* find in this chapter is a magic formula for changing other people into what you would like them to be. To solve the problems that concern you, therefore, you must change *your* attitude. If you handle your relationships with other people with the proper attitude, you will be able not only to solve your problems, but in many cases to keep them from coming up in the first place. You don't have to love or like everybody you're associated with in business; you just have to learn how to get along with them.

Developing the proper relationship with your executive's wife

Just as the proper relationship between executive and secretary is strictly professional, so the relationship of the secretary to his wife is strictly nonpersonal. There are exceptions to every rule, but in general the following suggestions will apply.

Wives of executives tend to be a little jealous of their husbands' secretaries for many reasons. The secretary spends almost as much time with the executive as his wife does, and by the very nature of her job understands and sympathizes with the problems of his work and shares his elation over his accomplishments and his successes. An executive is prone to speak highly of his secretary to others: "Ms. Jones is the best secretary in the world"; "I couldn't get along without Ms. Jones." But he is seldom so free in making similar statements about his wife. If the secretary is younger than the wife and also attractive, the problem is compounded. However, you can develop the proper relationship with your executive's wife and avoid many of the unhappy situations that occur all too often.

Your personal life, and especially your social life, should be completely separate and apart from the office. You have social interests and friends, and so does your executive— and seldom are they mutual (if for no other reason, because of the difference in income). There is no reason for, and many reasons against, dining with your executive and his family, either in public or as guests in the home, his or yours. Think of the reasons in favor of socializing with him and his wife, if you wish; we will consider here the reasons against.

Except in unusual circumstances (for example, his wife is a partner in the company or an officer in the corporation), your executive will be concerned with matters of business which are confidential and which he will not communicate even to his wife. A comptroller of a corporation I worked for once said of a matter which had supposedly been kept confidential within the organization "I don't know where the leak was, but my wife asked me about it last night—she heard it at a bridge party." Business matters which your executive considers confidential should not be communicated to any other person, even his wife. If your relationship with her is nonpersonal, this will pose no problem—she will not ask you; and if she does, you can simply plead ignorance of the matter.

The executive's wife should be treated with the courtesy accorded any other caller, in person or on the telephone. The one difference is that you may exercise your delegated authority in refusing admittance to an insistent visitor or in refusing to interrupt your executive for a persistent telephoner—unless the person is his wife. Don't argue with her; it's up to him to explain to her that you have instructions to see that he is not available, even to her, on occasion.

The wife who is jealous of the time her husband spends with his secretary will be doubly resentful of any overtime or evening work they do together. Plan your work to avoid overtime.

She would prefer that you be middle-aged and plain; if you are neither, she will like you better if you are conservative in both makeup and dress. Dress and behave with dignity in the office.

Just as with your executive, it is best not to be on a first-name basis with his wife. The "Dottie" and "Sally" relationship is more likely to lead to such problems as what to do when she criticizes him to you or before you, what to do when she quizzes you about his attention to another woman, what to do when she asks about the financial matters you handle for him. "Ms. X" helps to keep your relationship nonpersonal and discourages personal remarks and prying questions.

It behooves you to have her approve of you. If she doesn't, she may nag your boss to replace you until he finally does, just to keep peace at home.

The same advice applies in this section if your executive is a woman—except be *doubly* sure that your relationship with her husband is strictly nonpersonal.

Avoiding office feuds

Office feuds create more gray hair for executives than any other office problem. And in many cases, because certain women can't get along, the situation actually costs the company money.

Examples of this kind of problem are endless. We will look at a few of the most common. The first thing to do, of course, is to be sure that the secretary in the example is not *you*.

(1) The secretary who is overly conscious of her executive's position in the company—you could get an appointment to see the President of the United States with less effort than it takes to speak to her executive on the telephone. Take two secretaries with this attitude and you have a feuding female situation. Treat both her and her executive with the deference she believes they deserve, and, while you may never be good friends, you will at least be able to get along with her. If your executive has any objection to her attitude toward him, let him say so to her or to her executive.

(2) The secretary in a position of authority who has the right and the responsibility to request assistance, information, or action from you—and never lets you forget it. How nice it would be if women would hang together instead of separately! Although women, being the cats that we are, tend to credit women who have achieved a position of authority with anything but ability, nevertheless in most cases the woman has the job because of her *superior* ability. And she knows that in order to

keep that job she must continue to discharge her responsibilities effectively. Be sure that your attitude toward her is not one of grudging compliance but one of friendly and immediate cooperation. Give her the same support you would appreciate if you were in her position.

(3) The secretary in another office who always seems to be off from work because of illness when there is urgent work to be done in her office—and you inherit the job. It's easy and natural to resent this, especially if it happens very often, and can lead to a real feud unless you handle the situation properly. Don't assume that she's faking illness to have you do her work for her, and don't complain to her when she gets back to the office. If you are blessed with good health, thank God for it. But realize that some people, even though afflicted with nothing immediately fatal, do suffer from ailments that attack them from time to time making it next to impossible to perform on the job. Allergies can be incapacitating, arthritis can be agonizing, and viruses pick on some people more often than others. Do her work with the same meticulous care that you do your own, and tell her sincerely, when she returns to the office, that you hope she is feeling better. If doing her work really interferes with your own job, discuss the matter with your executive, not with her.

(4) The other secretary who shares your office but works for another executive—you work like a dog from nine to five, and she goofs off a good part of the time, either out at the water fountain or in the ladies' room, or talking on the telephone, and when she's out you have to answer her phone as well as your own. A situation like this is pretty hard to swallow, but feuding with her will only make it worse. Consider that she may be so well organized that she is actually accomplishing as much as you are, but with less effort. Tell yourself that your hard work will pay off in a raise or promotion and let her worry about her own professional future. In other words, mind your own business and be as friendly with her as you would if she were in a separate office and you wouldn't know how much time she spends out of it.

Developing the proper attitude
toward other people

Control of our behavior is much simpler if we have the proper attitude, but we can control our behavior even without the proper attitude. Good behavior can become a habit which will lead to the development of a changed attitude.

If we compare the philosophies of some of the world's greatest teachers and religious leaders, we find that all of them preach the golden rule: "Do unto others as you would have them do unto you." Getting along with people is as simple as that. Make a list of your business associates whom you particularly like, and then list the reasons why you like them. You will probably find such adjectives as friendly, considerate, cordial, honest, sincere, dependable, and the like. Now make a similar list of people you don't like, and the reasons why. This list of adjectives will contain just the opposite of the first one, and a few more besides. You believe they are rude, abrupt, inconsiderate, shallow, unreliable, unpleasant, overbearing, fawning, etc.

If you're playing the game this far, list adjectives that your associates might apply to you as attributed by the people who like you as well as those you have reason to believe don't like you. Remember, we don't have to *like* everybody, we just have to get along with them. If you have been completely honest in these two lists, you have a starting point from which to develop a proper attitude toward other people.

"People" is a general term used to mean two or more persons—and each person is an individual. To get along with people, therefore, we must learn to get along with individuals. It's easy and natural to respond to rudeness by being rude right back; to respond to an angry remark with an angry retort; to respond to a grumpy question with an equally grumpy reply. But it's also easy and natural to respond to those we like, who behave according to the reasons why we like them, in a similar manner. To change your attitude toward the people you don't like, the first step is to change your behavior toward them.

For example, practice "a soft answer turneth away wrath" the next time you have the occasion. You can make it work! It isn't easy to behave as we should with people who behave as they should *not*, but it pays off. Return a grumpy greeting with a smile and a pleasant reply; keep calm when someone else loses his temper; make a special effort to be nice to people you don't like; change your behavior and your attitude will change itself. Take the time and trouble to be friendly and courteous with all of your business associates, regardless of their position—from the janitor to the chairman of the board. Show Business has a saying that is equally applicable to the office: Be nice to the people you meet on the way up; you meet the same people on the way down.

How to give and take instructions

Problems frequently develop when instructions are involved. They arise because either the instructor or the instructee does not do a good job. First we will look at the proper way to give instructions.

As a secretary, you may need to give instructions to an assistant, a clerk in another office, or to someone outside the company. The instructions may range from a simple "type this" to complicated ones given to a printer concerning an advertising brochure. The proper way is the same, whether simple or complex.

Even if you give the same instructions to the same person a dozen times a day, such as "type this," they are much more palatable to the instructee if preceded by a "please." Be as explicit as necessary, but don't spell out every detail—give the other person credit for knowing something about what is to be done. "Please draft this, Margie. The boss wants to take ten copies of it to the meeting at 2:00." In a few words you are telling Margie to double space the typing and to reproduce at least ten copies before 2:00 this afternoon—which should be all she needs to know. This is much better than an abrupt "Margie, type this

in draft form and make ten copies right away." Margie will do
the job in either case, but her response will be better if you use
the first approach. Unless Margie has never typed a draft before,
an example of giving too much detail would be to add that the
copy is to be double spaced with two-inch margins, typed as an
original only, with the other copies to be made on the copy
machine.

When the instructions are complicated, be sure you
give sufficient information. Ask if the instructee has any questions before you leave her to her own initiative. A job that has to
be done over because the instructions were not clear is a waste
of time and money.

To reverse the situation, let's look at the proper way to
take instructions. Whether the instructor begins with a "please"
or not, be sure your manner is correct when you accept the task.
Be sure you have enough information to complete the assignment before you begin it, and perform it willingly. For example,
if you are Margie and your instructions are simply to "type this,"
you need more information. Draft or final form? How many
copies? When is it needed? To type a draft when it is ready to be
done in final form is a waste of time; to type it in final form when
a draft is wanted to make it easier for further revisions is also a
waste of time.

This example, while it is very simple, illustrates why it
is necessary that instructions be given and taken properly to
assure that what is wanted is understood by both the instructor
and the instructee. The objective is to get the job done efficiently.

How to give and take criticism

There is a saying that "Those who can, do; those who
can't, criticize." The word "criticism" immediately antagonizes
some people, but in this section we will look at criticism as a
very important and useful part of office procedure, an evaluation
of the merits and demerits of a piece of work.

You may be required, as a secretary, to review work done for your office by an assistant or by someone in another office. An example is a letter which has been prepared in another office for your executive's signature. Assume that there is no secretary's manual in your company to illustrate a uniform letter—each executive uses the style he prefers—and the secretary who typed the letter did not check with you before she prepared it. She used her own executive's style. When you review the letter, you note immediately that the salutation is "Dear Mr. Smith" instead of "Dear Harry" and that the complimentary close is "Sincerely yours" when your executive uses "Sincerely" only. The secretary is new and will probably be typing similar letters in the future, otherwise you might elect to retype the letter rather than speak to her about it.

Criticism is like "bad news" in a letter—it should be sandwiched; in other words, the pill should be sugar-coated. Remember that criticism considers merits as well as demerits. The demerit, that the letter will have to be retyped, can be sandwiched between a compliment on the merits of the letter and an offer to help the new girl. If her office is not too far away, you may want to return the letter in person. "Janet, this letter is a beautiful typing job. I'm sorry to have to ask you to retype it, but . . ." and explain the changes required. Then leave her with a friendly comment, such as "Please let me know if I can help you in any way until you learn your way around." Even though your personal opinion is that she should have been smart enough to check with you in the first place, it will serve no purpose to mention that. The objective of criticism is not to scold but to improve performance.

Taking criticism properly is just as important as giving it properly. If your critic does it properly, you will have no difficulty in accepting the criticism gracefully and making a mental note to be sure that you don't make the same mistake again. Assume that you are Janet, but instead of the situation in the foregoing example, something like this happens. The letter you prepared so carefully pops up in your in-basket a day or two later with the corrections indicated on the original and no other note of explanation. Subvert your natural inclination to resent the way your critic chose to call attention to your error; retype the letter and take it to her office. "I'm sorry you had to return the letter—I hope I've done it right this time." Be cordial and friendly and she is likely to respond in the same way.

What to do about office gossip

There are two kinds of office gossip: Rumors and speculations about office matters, and juicy tid-bits regarding personalities. There are those who create, perpetrate, or deprecate office gossip—a good secretary should be in the latter group.

Gossips, contrary to what men would have us believe, are not always women. In fact, some of the worst gossips are men, and this is especially true in an office. You, as a good secretary, do not gossip, so in this section we will see how we can discourage gossip on the part of others. First we will look at rumors and speculations about office matters.

Gossip is quite often started by the individual it concerns. The vice-president in charge of sales lets it be known that he is leaving the company to take a higher position with another organization, and speculation immediately begins about his replacement. Any time a vacancy occurs in an organization, from the bottom to the top level, those who are directly concerned or just plain nosy will have comments to make and opinions to voice. Your best bet is to say nothing and, if possible, to avoid listening to any of the speculations. There is really no need to concern yourself about what will happen "if" a certain person gets the job. Unless you are appointing the replacement, your speculations or preferences will have no bearing on who gets the job.

Gossip, especially on office matters that directly concern your own executive, is absolutely taboo for you. There are secretaries, not very good ones, who can't resist wanting to be "in the know" about everything. They may ask you leading questions about matters concerning your office, but no business of theirs, and in turn imply that they are prepared to exchange information. Avoid them like the plague; they cause nothing but trouble, and you may wind up involved in it. Simply say "I don't know," when you're questioned. To imply that you know, but are not at liberty to say, encourages further prying.

Juicy tid-bits regarding personalities spread like wildfire, and this type of gossip is also usually generated by the one it concerns. Personal affairs should be kept completely separate from business, yet there are those who can't resist confiding to an office associate a personal matter that has nothing to do with work. Items of personal gossip that should never be repeated include these: an imminent divorce, someone is sleeping around, a co-worker has a son, or daughter, on drugs, hanky-panky between two people who are married, but not to each other. Keep your mind open and your mouth shut; you may need the favor returned sometime.

How to solve an office problem when it's your responsibility

Problem solving can be reduced to a simple formula, and that formula can be applied to any given situation. A secretary is not likely to be called upon to solve a problem which has international implications, or even one that could shake a corporation to its Board of Directors, but an everyday problem involving a snippy secretary across the hall can be solved with the same formula used in much more complicated situations.

What sort of office problems would a secretary be called upon to solve? There may be problems related to the executive-secretary relationship, secretary-secretary, secretary-stenographer, or secretary-typist association, or among a group of stenographers or typists the secretary supervises. Let's consider the logical steps in problem solving:

1. Identify the problem.
2. Get the relevant facts.

3. Involve as few people as possible.

4. Consider all possible alternatives.

5. Select the solution that does the least harm to the fewest people.

If responsibility for solving the problem or making the necessary decision is yours, take care of it alone if possible. If you put the responsibility on your executive, the personnel department, or any other individual or department, you are failing to discharge your duty.

A good general rule is to look at the end result desired and adopt the best means to achieve it. Be realistic about the price to be paid—we usually have to lose a little to gain a little more. There need not be a winner and a loser in every contest. If a satisfactory compromise will get the job done, make it.

Some people refuse to make a decision in the hope that the problem will go away. This is wishful thinking; they fail to realize that to do nothing means that they *have* made a decision—to do nothing.

How and when to ask for a raise

Good management practices usually call for a review of a secretary's performance on a periodic basis and a discussion between the supervisor and supervised at that time. Depending upon the supervisor's evaluation, the secretary is rewarded with an increase in pay on the basis of merit, denied an increase because of mediocre performance, or warned that if deficiencies are not corrected within a certain period she may be replaced. If you think you were overlooked when the merit increases were awarded, first examine your own performance.

Are you the best secretary in the organization? Maybe, in your opinion, but perhaps you have not considered all the facts. A good secretary is prompt, dependable, loyal, efficient, has a good sense of humor and gets along with everybody—and a good many other things as well. But remember that the company must be making more money from your service than you are paid for your job. If you have reached the saturation point in your contribution to the company, you have, so to speak, "hit the ceiling" for your job.

Asking "How about a raise?" is not very likely to get you one. Lead into the discussion gradually and at a carefully chosen time—when you believe your executive is in a receptive mood. Ask if he has time to discuss your work, and if he has, begin by asking if there is any way you can do a better job for him. Keep the discussion frank and objective, and if he shocks you by listing ways you can improve, swallow the rest of your prepared remarks and work to fulfill his expectations before you broach the subject again. On the other hand, if he says you are the world's greatest secretary and he could not survive in the business world without your help, admit that you agree with him and that is why you wonder why your paycheck does not reflect some of his enthusiasm.

Never ask for a raise on the basis of what "someone else" makes. Even people who are doing "exactly" the same job may discharge their duties with a difference significant enough to warrant a difference in rate of pay.

Don't ask for a raise on the basis of need. Management is operating a business, not a charity, and should not be expected to give you an increase in salary because your children are in college, your husband is out of work, or you have to put your mother in a rest home.

Any employee must be worth more to the company than the salary paid; that is, the company must make money on the labor dollar to maximize its profit margin. One way a secretary can assure progress to the top of her profession is to increase her contribution to the company profit margin.

If you really believe that you are underpaid for the kind of job performance you are giving to management, don't threaten to quit—until you find another job that will pay you a salary you consider commensurate with your ability. And don't threaten to quit unless you mean it. You may find that option no longer open to you if you change your mind.

What to do when you are offered a promotion

Accept it? Not always! The secretarial field is one of personal service, and personalities are deeply involved in an executive-secretary relationship. The best secretary in the world to one person can be an abysmal failure to another. And money, or even position, is not everything. A living wage earned in a job which is a pleasure, working for a person with whom you have rapport, is a much better job situation than working for a tyrannical autocrat at a high salary if you wind up at the end of every day with jangled nerves and a handful of tranquilizers.

Another type of promotion which may not be all that it seems at first is a change in the kind of work. For example, if you are a secretary and enjoy secretarial work, think carefully before you accept a promotion to head of the word processing center or chief of the purchasing department.

On the other hand, be alert to opportunities for promotion and be prepared so that if another job is offered and you believe it would indeed be a satisfactory promotion, accept it, and good luck! But be sure you vacate your old position leaving goodwill behind you. Tidy up the loose ends, be as helpful as you can to your replacement, and stand ready to be consulted by phone or in person if you can be of any help during the first few weeks of the changeover. Never leave a job without adequate notice. A good rule to follow is always leave a job with the idea that you may want to go back sometime—and that you would be welcome.

How to avoid the rut of complacency

Seniority means something in unions, but it means less in management and administration. Too often, people, including secretaries, believe they are indispensable simply because they have held the same job for a number of years. This is not the case—nobody is indispensable, not even a top-notch secretary.

Avoid secretarial obsolescence. Read articles and magazines in secretarial, management, and administrative publications on the latest developments in your field. The prescribed way to write a letter today is obsolete tomorrow. Spelling, terminology, and phraseology change periodically. Keeping up with your field is not enough—keep ahead of it. Enroll in a formal course or two in night school or a college or university. Study not only courses in business which are related to your office responsibilities, but take a course or two in the field of your executive or your company: real estate, engineering, marketing, anatomy. Keep your mind alert through enough formal study to keep your wits sharp. Don't exhibit the signs of middle age by resisting change: age is a state of mind—anticipate change, and be ready for it.

Some examples of complacent secretaries who wake up too late include one whose executive for the last 15 years suddenly drops dead—and his replacement has his own secretary; one whose executive retires, and his job, as well as hers, is simply abolished; one whose ambitious young executive accepts a transfer across the country and never gives a thought to offering her an opportunity to transfer with him. In the changing business world today, nothing can be taken for granted. Even presidents of corporations can be fired, and so can obsolete secretaries.

Keeping family and job
in the proper perspective

People who work for a living, and today that includes almost everybody from 16 to 60, lead a double life: One life on the job, and the other away from it. From nine to five, the office comes first; except in unusual circumstances, a secretary should devote off hours to personal business and forget the office.

Arrange your personal life so that you can devote your complete attention to your job. For example, if you have children or other dependent relatives such as an ailing mother or husband, arrange for their adequate care while you are on the job. Personal calls from home to the office should be discouraged except in case of emergency. Your calls from the office to check on personal business should likewise be limited and, if possible, should be made on your own time, during lunch or a coffee break.

Executives will be appropriately sympathetic if your work is interrupted by a genuine emergency at home: "Billy fell down the basement steps and split his head open!" But not very many are willing to pay a full-time salary for a part-time employee. Have it understood with members of your family that you are not to be disturbed at the office unless it is absolutely necessary. Examples of some types of calls that should be discouraged are these:

1. Mama, who lives alone, calls to chat for as long as you are willing to talk. Tell Mama that you will call her later from home.

2. Billy calls to complain that the housekeeper won't let him play baseball. Tell Billy to mind the housekeeper and you'll talk about it when you get home.

3. Sally calls to tell you what she did in school today. Unless something really spectacular happened, this kind of conversation can be saved for the evening when all members of the family are present.

4. The housekeeper calls with a minor problem about dinner. Delegate to her minor decisions with regard to running the house, such as buying ground chuck if the ground beef doesn't look too good today.

Husbands are not as likely as wives to call the office to chat; however, if you have one who does, turn him off. Handle a necessary personal call as quickly as possible and get back to doing what you're paid for.

On the other hand, your time at home belongs to you and your family and friends. When you leave the office, leave it and its problems with the company. If you have managed your work day properly, you should arrive at home with the necessary energy and enthusiasm to take up the other part of your double life. Whatever your family responsibilities are, discharge them with the same attention to detail that you employ at the office. There may be occasions to plead exhaustion from a day at the office, but they should not occur often. Plan your personal life so that you have time to listen to the children when they want to talk about what they did at school today; time to discuss finances and other personal matters with your husband; time for an occasional evening out; and time to plan weekends or vacations with your family.

Women are in a unique position today. We can be both a career woman and a housewife—there is no longer a need to choose one or the other. Plan your time wisely, keep personal business outside the company and company business inside the office, and you should enjoy a successful and happy double life.

Chapter 13

NINE RULES FOR
GETTING COOPERATION

THERE ARE OFFICE PROBLEMS even among those who are working toward the same goal with the proper attitude of cooperation and assistance. At any given time, however, either in the course of your routine work or upon direct instructions from your executive, you may be required to obtain information or assistance from a person who is not exactly cooperative.

Uncooperative people are usually suspicious, antagonistic, and negative in their attitudes, and fall roughly into two groups: Those who are known to you before you make the initial contact, and those who become known to you (an unwelcome surprise) after the initial contact. These people automatically respond to a request for help with a complaint about the work involved, a detailed account of other responsibilities which have priority over your request, or a dozen reasons why your request poses a problem. They may even begin with a flat "no." Uncooperative people range in attitude from those who are mildly negative to those who are practically immovable. The amount of effort required to secure the necessary cooperation will vary in direct proportion to the amount of resistance to be overcome.

Your job is to consider the end result desired, and then do whatever is necessary to achieve it. The last resort is to report a failure to your boss; you are returning to him a duty he delegated to you.

It may be difficult, but you can obtain information or assistance from a person who is reluctant to provide it. You will need patience, understanding, and perseverance. Following these rules may help:

1. Specialize your request for cooperation.
2. Realize why a person is basically uncooperative.
3. Select the proper person to approach.
4. Be sure you are communicating.
5. Be sure your own attitude is one of cooperation.
6. Use cooperation-getting words and phrases.
7. React with reason rather than emotion.
8. Accept blame for an error that isn't even yours.
9. Be appreciative and give credit when it's due.

Each rule is explained and then an example is given to show how to apply the nine rules to obtain a positive response from one whose first reaction is negative.

Specialize your request for cooperation

Specialize your request for cooperation if you have learned from past experience that you will very likely meet with a negative response. Put that person in the category of people who must be "handled with kid gloves"—with a basically un-cooperative person, ordinary courtesy won't get the job done.

Although lengthy discussions of personal matters are tabu in the office, there are occasions when personal comments can be used effectively to carry out your responsibilities. In dealing with a person you know will have to be cajoled into doing what you ask (even if it is a part of her job), begin the conversation with the idea of putting her in the proper state of mind—friendly and agreeable. "I'll bet you're proud of your son—I just heard he made Eagle Scout." "I'm sorry to hear your mother is in the hospital." But be sincere in your interest and give her an opportunity to comment before you go ahead with your request. The few seconds spent on a personal matter may in the long run cut the total time required to get the cooperation you need.

Pay a sincere compliment on her work, especially if you can quote your executive. "Mr. Smith was delighted with the excellent report you compiled on sales during the first quarter." Or, "Mr. Smith was really pleased that you sent him the information for the Board meeting a day early." If you can't quote him, think of something on your own. "You did a marvelous job of typing that statistical report." "You must have an infallible filing system; I can always count on you to produce a copy of something I can't find anywhere else."

Now that you have "mellowed" your target, you can get down to business.

Realize why a person is basically uncooperative

There is always a reason why a person is basically uncooperative. One with a negative attitude may have a problem which is either physical or emotional, or perhaps a combination of both. She may have a feeling of inferiority with regard to her job, her title, or her salary. She may have personal problems at home which she can't forget when she comes to the office. She may have a health problem which is a nagging inconvenience but not serious enough to keep her away from the job. You as a secretary are not expected to be able to diagnose an individual's particular problem, but you should recognize that one exists.

Make no attempt to psychoanalyze another person, however; any effort on your part to do so is quite likely to do more harm than good.

You are not expected to like everybody or to understand everybody; you are only expected to "get along" with them as required to discharge your duties. You should remember that every person wants to be admired and respected, to be recognized as an individual, and to be treated with the dignity to which any human being is entitled. Not many of us are problem-free, but as long as we can cope with our problems we are considered "adjusted" to the world around us. One with a negative attitude is less well adjusted, and this should be taken into consideration when you receive a negative response, a curt reply, or an angry retort. Persevere and adjust your own attitude accordingly, remembering that your objective is to get what you're after—cooperation. You must persuade the negative, uncooperative individual to change her attitude to one of positive cooperation. And note that *you* cannot change her attitude— only she can do that.

Select the proper person to approach

Selecting the proper person to approach is important even if you have every reason to expect instant success. This is even more important if the one who will ultimately respond to your request has a negative attitude. This applies whether you are dealing with another office or department in your own company or with an outside company.

Go only as high as necessary on the organization chart to get the help you need. You're wasting an executive's time if you make your request to the head of the department when his secretary can handle the matter. Furthermore, by "going over her head," you will alienate the one who is directed by her supervisor to supply the information you're after.

On the other hand, if you begin with a secretary or the person who usually handles such matters, you are much more likely to get a favorable response and immediate action. If she is not able to act on her own initiative, she will refer you to someone who can help you or perhaps offer to obtain the information for you from the proper person in her department. In any case, she will be pleased that you consulted her first.

A good general rule to follow is to stay on your own relative level on the organization chart. A secretary-to-secretary or secretary-to-clerk request is much better than secretary-to-executive. To state your request to the secretary serves two purposes: She will appreciate your assuming she will have the answer, whether she does or not, and she will realize that you are observing proper protocol in trying to save her executive's time. It is certainly true that many times a request is made to an executive who then explains the situation to the secretary and asks her to take care of the matter. Try the secretary first; if she can't help you, she will let you know if you should talk to someone else.

Be sure you are communicating

Communication means the transfer or exchange of information and therefore involves two or more things or people. Be sure your request is understood. Note that we "request," not "demand." A soft voice, friendly words, and a pleasant introduction to your problems are likely to elicit a sympathetic reaction. On the other hand, a demand or an accusation delivered in a critical manner can result in instant antagonism that will get you nowhere. Anyone would prefer to consider a request rather than to comply with a command. Avoid giving the impression that you are ordering, directing, or demanding, or that your executive is doing so.

For two people to communicate, one must talk and the other must listen—and you can't do both at the same time. You are not communicating if you speak and then tune out the other person while you think over what you have just said and what you're going to say next. When you listen, listen for the meaning of what is said and not for what you want to hear, and don't interrupt or cut her off before she has completed what she has to say. If you do, she will conclude that you think her comments are unimportant and she will resent it.

Continue the discussion only long enough to obtain a favorable response; but be sure you are not abrupt in terminating the conversation. Add a note of genuine appreciation for whatever help you have been able to obtain—and take your leave on a friendly note.

Be sure your own attitude is one of cooperation

A person I know frequently says "She just won't cooperate with me," but what she really means is "She won't do as I say." Cooperation means to work together, and therefore it takes more than one person to cooperate. The secretary who is asking for cooperation, therefore, must herself be cooperative.

Your initial request should be made with the normal courtesy you extend to any business contact unless you believe it necessary to "specialize" according to Rule 1. Your own manner in requesting help from another will determine, in part, the response you receive. If you are not known to the other person, identify yourself and your executive by name and company or department, and by title if that seems appropriate. If you know her name, use it; if you don't know her name and she does not offer it, ask for it and write it down so that you *will* know it the next time—and be sure to pronounce it properly.

Make your request in a straightforward manner as though you expect a favorable response. If your request is reasonable, within her realm of responsibility to grant it, and in accordance with company policy, you may expect a simple concurrence with no further discussion. However, even in these circumstances, you may meet with a negative response. In that case, your attitude in further conversation becomes even more important.

Pay attention to tone of voice as well as words. Many times it's not what you say, it's the way you say it. Be sure that your tone matches your words and conveys the proper meaning. To check yourself on how the tone of your voice can convey as much meaning as your words, try the simple sentence "I'm sorry about that" and say it with sincerity, then try it with sarcasm, frivolity, and irritation. Think of the difference in attitude that would be elicited by each of the "tones" you have used.

Be sure you maintain the proper attitude at all times. Think the proper attitude, the proper phrases, and the proper tone. Think friendship, cooperation, and success, and cultivate a "voice with a smile."

Use cooperation-getting words and phrases

When you make your request, use cooperation-getting words and phrases. Use the name of your executive; after all, you want the information because he wants it and has asked you to get it. An employee is likely to react more favorably to a request made in the name of an executive than to one made by an employee on her own level. But remember to *request* in his name, not demand. "Mr. Smith would like a special financial report." You're asking for the information not for yourself, but to keep Mr. Smith happy. "Could you please" and "he will appreciate" will encourage a friendly response.

Ask for advice—she will like this, especially if she has a feeling of insecurity about her job. "You're experienced in these matters, what do you suggest?" This indicates that you respect her ability. If you have had a prior similar contact, refer to it. "The last time I talked with you, we were not able to work out a solution—I hope this time we will be more successful." Or, "The last time we had a problem, you came to the rescue—we hope you can help us again."

React with reason rather than emotion

Secretaries engage in role-playing all the time and frequently have a preconceived notion of how a conversation is going before it is begun. If you have a travel reservation to make for your executive, you have a mental picture of the routine before you take any action at all. You envision telephoning the travel office and in a matter of minutes receiving confirmation of a round-trip reservation to Washington on the flights requested. But what happens when the wanted reservations are not available? Too often, when our preconceived mental picture goes awry, we react with emotion rather than reason.

An old saw for holding your temper in check is "Count to ten before you say anything." When you hit a stone wall in your effort to get something done, no useful purpose will be served by "blowing your stack." Count to ten, then consider alternatives. Be reasonable and understanding, and accept the best alternative gracefully. In the case of reservations, if they aren't available as requested, don't blame the travel office, the travel clerk, or even the airline. The blame, if any, is yours for not calling earlier.

There is no difficulty in maintaining a good disposition when things go your way, but it takes work to keep from losing it when people or things are uncooperative. Arguments or disagreements occur only when two or more people participate; to avoid arguments and disagreements, then, simply do not participate. A natural emotional reaction to an accusation or a cutting remark is to reply in kind. But then what happens? Bad feeling on both sides. React with reason rather than emotion, and respond graciously. "I'm very sorry . . .," and watch the tone! Do this for two reasons: One, there will be bad feeling on only one side; and two, if you really want to get even with one who has made a cutting remark, be nice to her—that will make her ashamed of her behavior.

In dealing with uncooperative people, you can expect negative responses, brusque remarks, and possibly even rough language. Remember, though, if you have a job to do, it's up to you to keep the conversation going until you get what you're after. React with reason rather than emotion and you will be able to maintain your own proper attitude of cooperation.

Accept blame for an error that isn't even yours

If your request to someone with a negative attitude has to do with an error which has been made, accept some of the responsibility if at all possible, even if none of the fault is yours. She will be grateful for your sharing the blame, and it will make her feel less guilty for having goofed. You won't lose anything; and if you help her to save face, you may gain a friend.

In almost any situation you will be able to find something you could have done better or sooner or more carefully. If so, say so. Use the editorial "we" if you can't honestly think of a single action (or lack of it) on your part that might have prevented the error. "We should have caught the mistake before the letter went out" (even though the letter had not crossed your desk). Or, "We should have checked the figures on the adding machine before we typed the report" (even if the report had been typed before you saw it).

In any case, if an error is involved, avoid accusation or pinpointing blame. And of course *never* put any of the blame on your executive.

Be appreciative and give credit when it's due

Be genuinely appreciative for the cooperation you have received, even though it may have been earned only after a long, hard battle. "Thank you very much for your help." "Mr. Smith wanted me to tell you how much he appreciates what you have done for us." Do this for two reasons: One, it's good manners; and two, it's groundwork for the next time you need help from the same person.

If there is any opportunity at all to give credit for a job well done, do it, and with a smile. You never know when someone may have a feeling that she "doesn't get credit for anything." "Mr. Smith asked me to thank you for typing that rush letter so quickly. It was a beautiful job." And, if you have an opportunity, make a complimentary remark about her work to someone else who may repeat it. What you say *about* a person carries more weight with her than what you say *to* her.

The credit you give is quite likely to pay dividends; credit that you fail to give will be held against you indefinitely.

The uncooperative person may be anybody: The shipping clerk, the travel agent, the head of purchasing, etc. If you will follow these rules in dealing with people with a negative attitude, and persevere, you will not only achieve your objective of the moment but quite likely you will find that subsequent requests, following the same rules each time, may eventually result in willing cooperation at the first approach.

To summarize, the rules are:

1. Specialize your request for cooperation.
2. Realize why a person is basically uncooperative.
3. Select the proper person to approach.
4. Be sure you are communicating.
5. Be sure your own attitude is one of cooperation.
6. Use cooperation-getting words and phrases.
7. React with reason rather than emotion.
8. Accept blame for an error that isn't even yours.
9. Be appreciative and give credit when it's due.

Chapter 14

REFLECTING AN IMPRESSIVE IMAGE FOR YOUR MANAGER AND YOUR COMPANY

PUBLIC RELATIONS FOR YOUR MANAGER AND YOUR COMPANY is not restricted to, although it includes, your contacts with people outside the company. While it is very important that you project to customers, clients, and others outside the company the proper image of your manager and his organization, it is equally important that you maintain good public relations *within* the company. Fortunately, the guidelines for creating good public relations for your manager are the same for either situation.

A good personality is not essential for good public relations, although it helps. If you are an outgoing person, meet people easily, like most of them, and have no difficulty in communicating, you may be naturally good at public relations. However, even if you do not have a natural PR personality, you can develop one which will be adequate for your responsibilities to your manager and your company.

Like the "you" approach in letter-writing, a good public relations representative will subjugate "I" and "we" to "you" and "your." In general, the checklist below separates what you should be from what you should not be:

Be	*Don't be*
Friendly	Fawning, cold, overly familiar
Courteous	Obsequious, impolite, downright rude
Pleasant	Brusque, abrupt, curt
Helpful	Officious

Keeping visitors to your office happy

As a secretary, greeting visitors to your office is only a part of your duties, and normally you will not be expected to entertain the visitor, whether he is calling to see you or your manager. (Generic "he"; the same applies if the visitor is a woman.) On the other hand, a visitor should be greeted the moment he enters the office, assuming that you are there when he arrives. Put yourself in his place and recall how annoying it can be to enter another office on a business errand and be ignored in any one of the following situations:

1. The secretary is on the telephone and continues her conversation without so much as looking your way.
2. The secretary is talking with another obviously personal visitor in her office about which color of draperies will look best with a flowered couch and makes no attempt to interrupt herself.
3. The secretary is typing at a great clip and ignores your presence until she comes to the end of the page.

In your own case, you would perhaps be willing to wait a moment for a telephone call or a personal conversation to be terminated or for a page of typing to be completed; however, you would at least appreciate an acknowledgment of your presence when you enter the office.

When a visitor enters your office and you are on the telephone, at least nod to him with a friendly smile, interrupt your conversation if you possibly can, at least long enough to tell him you will "be with him in a moment." You should not be chit-chatting with another secretary in the first place; but if you are, company business takes precedence over personal business. Terminate the conversation at once and take care of the visitor.

Unless your manager is awaiting your typed page with bated breath, take care of the visitor and *then* complete your typing project.

In many cases you can "dispose" of a visitor in a moment by giving him a bit of information he needs, ushering him into your executive's office, or making an appointment for him later. If he wants to discuss something with you that will take more than just a moment and you have something to do for your executive which is, in your opinion, more important than what the visitor wants to discuss, explain the situation courteously. "I must finish this first; would you like to wait a few minutes, or come back later?" Or "I'm on a rush job for Mr. Smith which he needs by noon. Could you come back after lunch?"

A visitor from outside the company, depending upon your executive's instructions, may require additional attention once you have greeted him and determined the purpose of his call. You may be expected to direct him to the coffee machine or offer to get a cup for him. You may be required only to ask him to be seated and help himself to a magazine until your executive is able to see him. Your greeting should be cordial and pleasant, regardless of whether your executive considers him a pest and a bore, and regardless of whether you agree.

Conversation with a visitor should be limited, on your part, to obtaining or checking his name and company affiliation, and the subject of the business he is to discuss with your executive. In requesting this information, be courteous and matter of fact; do not pry in an effort to learn more than you need.

How to give a "no" answer tactfully

Here you can apply the same rules for writing a "bad news" letter. "Sandwich" the negative reply between two positives. "Thank you for calling our office; we appreciate your thinking of us. I'm truly sorry we can't help you, but try us again—perhaps we can do better next time."

Remember to be just as courteous to people within the company as you are to present or potential customers or clients. "I appreciate and sympathize with your problem. I understand your need for an exception in this case, but I can think of no way to get around that particular company policy. Perhaps you can make arrangements to . . ." When you really can be of no help and must give a negative reply, try to suggest another avenue, if you possibly can, another person or office, for example. Even if the suggestion you make results in another negative, your own reply will be reinforced and the disappointment to the requester will be divided instead of directed 100 percent to your office.

When you are being genuinely helpful to another person, that is, you are satisfying his request (the "yes" answer), you have no problem in being friendly, courteous, and polite. When your answer must be negative, patience is a required virtue because all too often the person being refused is prone to argue. Don't shut off a person who wants to argue the point, even if he becomes completely unreasonable. Stick to your guns, keep your patience and your aplomb, and let him blow his stack. It's better to let him "get it out of his system" rather than have him nurse a grudge toward your office. And the next time your paths cross, be as pleasant as though the incident had never happened.

The customer or client is a guest of the company and is always treated with courtesy and consideration. He is right even when he is wrong; regardless of his attitude, the secretary retains her composure and controls her temper and her tongue.

How your health affects your work

An efficient secretary is a healthy one, and unless you have a health problem which creates for you a partial or temporary disability beyond your control, you should be able to maintain a relatively low absentee rate because of illness.

Basic good health depends upon good health habits: Balanced diet, adequate physical exercise, sufficient sleep, and cleanliness. Many years ago, women were continually suffering from the "vapors," but apparently that ailment was caused, in part, by tight corsets—the vapors and corsets went out at about the same time. This is not to say that today's woman does not suffer from wearing foundations which are too tight—some do, but should not. A tight girdle does not eliminate lumps and bulges, it merely rearranges them. The sensible way to keep your measurements within reasonable bounds is to eat properly and exercise regularly.

Adequate and satisfactory sleep promotes bright eyes and a clear skin. Adequate sleep varies from person to person, but generally ranges from five to ten hours a night. Determine your own requirement and establish your schedule accordingly.

Cleanliness also has different meanings for different people. For some, morning and evening showers or baths are routine; others, especially those with dry-skin problems, settle with much less on the advice of a dermatologist. Some people wash their hair at least once a day; others are content to do so every week or two. Determine the best schedule for you, based upon your own skin type and hair texture. Bathe and wash your hair often enough to maintain a clean, well-groomed look, but don't overdo it—if your skin is dry, you may develop scales that shed like dandruff, and if your hair is dry, too many shampoos will make it look like a fright wig.

One of the myths about women, which has been dispelled by a comparison of statistics, is that women who work tend to have a higher absentee rate, because of illness, than men. With the present medical aids available, women no longer have any reason to take "the usual" two days of sick leave every month, and for one who is menopausal, hormones and estrogens will keep her on the job.

A secretary owes it to her executive to be on the job unless she has asked in advance, and been granted, permission to be excused—for personal business, vacation, or what have you. An exception is when she is ill. When you let him know at nine in the morning that you won't be able to report to work because of illness, his entire day must be reorganized. Before you let him down unexpectedly, be sure that you are genuinely ill—not that you "just don't feel like going to work."

On the other hand, if you *are* genuinely ill, especially if you have a temperature and feel as though you're "coming down with something," by all means stay *away* from the office and do your executive and everybody else a favor. The company doesn't need a martyr who comes to work with communicable disease and spreads it throughout the office staff.

You may be genuinely ill without carrying contagious germs; for example, you are suffering from a slight virus but have no temperature, you have a migraine headache, your arthritis is acting up, or you have a back problem. (None of these ailments is caused by age, by the way.) Stay home and recuperate before you return to the office.

Your health does indeed affect your work and your efficiency. If you feel well and attack your work every morning with the day's goal in mind, you can turn out a mountain of work with a minimum of effort and leave the office at the end of the day with a sense of satisfaction and with vigor left over. When you spend your day at work longing to be home in bed, staring at each piece of paper to muster the energy to attack the job it calls for, waiting for the time you can drag your weary bones away from the office, you are cheating the company. You are taking a day's pay for a half-day's work, and it may take you a week to straighten out the slips and errors you let get by because you were operating at about 50 percent efficiency.

Take care of yourself and promote your job security. Your executive can count on you to run the office when he is away, but he depends upon you to be there, whether he is or not.

Proper dress for the office

Proper dress for the office is always on the conservative side, regardless of what is currently *haute couture*. A few selected quality garments for the office are preferred over a variety of inexpensive copies of current "in" fashions. The professional secretary will strive for an elegant, understated look.

Any fashion expert will recommend that you accentuate your good features and disguise your bad ones; just don't accentuate your good ones in the office if they are best saved for after five. Even after five, a fashion director once gave this advice: "Whatever you expose, be sure it's good looking." You've exposed too much when you've attracted more attention in the office because of your physical attributes rather than your capability in discharging your duties.

Selection of business dress should be made on the basis of comfort (good fit) and suitability. Clothing should be durable—that is, not wilted by noon. Check carefully the labels on the clothing you choose for the office and be sure the fabric is wrinkle- and sag-proof, preferably also washable.

Although most office jobs are relatively sedentary, the chief complaint of secretaries is aching feet. This problem can cause not only a waspish disposition, but also a drawn and haggard look. Some women suffer on the way to and from work in beautiful but painful shoes—and don "fuzzy-wuzzies" in the office! Bedroom slippers have no place in the office, nor do "sneakers." Select your shoes for comfort—and be sure they fit.

Clothes worn underneath are more important than those worn for the business world to see—especially to the secretary. The support provided by undergarments designed for that purpose can make the difference, at the end of the day, between (1) dragging a drooping body home to the living room couch or (2) a springing exit from the office, ready for dinner out and an evening on the town. Proper foundation garments are very important to the woman who spends a great deal of her time sitting. They encourage proper posture at a desk or office machine, which means less fatigue over a period of time. They also contribute to an attractive appearance in face as well as figure—when body muscles sag, facial muscles also tend to droop.

Standards of office dress are dictated, in part, as a matter of safety. In the office, jewelry is simple and in good taste. Necklaces should be short and plain; pins may vary in size.

Bracelets, if any, should be quiet (no tinkling bangles or charms). Dangling necklaces or bracelets can become entangled in office equipment; broken beads rolling about an office floor are as dangerous as an unexpected roller skate. Full skirts are a safety hazard if the hem is caught by the heel of a shoe or the caster on a chair.

With regard to shopping, two pieces of advice are worth remembering: (1) be sure that, whatever you buy, you are convinced that you look absolutely scrumptious in it, and (2) shop only when you don't *need* anything. In other words, buy only what *you* believe is best for you, not what a particularly aggressive saleswoman talks you into buying.

Hair should be arranged in a becoming style which is neat and easily kept. Extreme styles are reserved for evening glamour. A "hair-do" for tonight may be a "hair-don't" for the office tomorrow. Settle this problem by having a short cut if your face can stand it, and wear a wig or hairpiece for a public appearance after five.

Fingernails should be long enough to protect the finger tips, but not long enough to dig clams. Nail polish is optional. Dark red or silver-white polish should be avoided in the office; pastels are more suitable.

A professional secretary should "smell" only one way: clean. Distinctive perfume, cologne, even bath oil, can activate other people's allergies. Your executive may not hesitate to request that you leave the perfume for after five; but be equally considerate of visitors to the office who may also suffer—in silence.

A friend of mine once described a woman in her sixties as a charming, beautiful and exciting person. "With her," he said, "age is only an adjective." A secretary should be ageless, because age should make no difference in her efficiency—this works from both ends of the scale. A younger girl should give the impression of a certain amount of maturity, and the woman who is indeed mature should carefully avoid giving the impression of obsolescence. A career secretary should lean toward neither teenage fashion not yet grandmotherly styles, regardless of her age.

Developing the proper attitude toward your job

Do you wake up every morning eager to get to the job? Do you bounce into the office and dive into yesterday's leftovers and today's projects with vigor and enthusiasm? If not, take a good look at your job.

Some people face anything at 9:00 in the morning with a zero degree of enthusiasm; "night people" may check in the office at around nine and don't really know what's going on until noon—they do their best work in the afternoon, and never go to bed until midnight. Others get up with the sun, accomplish great things before noon, and begin to deteriorate after lunch, gradually declining to a ten o'clock bedtime. If you are a nine to fiver, you must be a "day person" or learn to develop into one. In short, you must be alert from the time you get to the office until you leave.

Assuming that you can begin the day with an attitude reflecting "Hello, you beautiful world," you should greet the office with the same cheery mood. This will be easy if you like your executive, you like your work, and you think your company is the greatest in the world. When you are unhappy with any component, you may be in the wrong job—and the time to discover that is early in your career. "Job hopping" is accomplished much more successfully and with less sacrifice on your part when you are a novice in the business world than when you have accumulated several years of company service credit and fringe benefits. In effect, you lose your freedom of choice when you have been in the same job for several years—your decisions are dictated by considerations other than job description, title, or salary.

Evaluate your job, and your attitude toward it, objectively. If you find that you consider your job a drag and can't wait to get through each day or each week, check to be sure that the heart of the problem is *not* your attitude. Reasons why people have a less-than-enthusiastic attitude toward their job include these:

1. Lack of understanding concerning the need for the duties performed; just how does your job fit into the overall company objectives? If you don't know the answer to this question, find out!

2. Lack of knowledge, resulting in uncertainty regarding your effectiveness; any time you are hesitant about your competence in your job, look to outside assistance—read up on the literature (there is written material on every conceivable subject) or take a formal course at any level for which you are qualified (high school, business school, adult education or university).

3. No chance for advancement. Assume that you are secretary to the Chairman of the Board of a small corporation, the top secretarial job in the organization. Don't lag up and be content where you are. If you're capable enough, you may end up Corporate Secretary. When there is no apparent chance for advancement, look around and create your own.

4. Non-challenging job—you are overqualified and can do your present job in your sleep. Sleep through the day with your eyes open to other opportunities, within or outside the company. Remember that lack of a challenge in your daily job will lead to deterioration of your present capabilities.

Since you spend about a third of each working day on the job, you should make every effort to make sure you enjoy it. Before you take the drastic step of looking for another job, be sure you have exhausted all possibilities for developing the proper attitude toward the one you have.

How improving your personal appearance can improve your personality

Behavior and personal appearance are closely related. The individual who has a pleasant manner seems attractive to others, and one who feels that she *is* attractive is more likely to be pleasant to others. Conversely, an unattractive appearance and a contrary disposition are frequently found in the same person. An employer may assume that a neat personal appearance indicates that neat work may be expected, whereas a sloppy appearance may mean sloppy work habits as well.

Secretaries are seldom employed, or promoted, on the basis of looks alone. Other qualifications being equal, however, the more attractive package of the required skills and capabilities will be selected. Not all women can be beautiful, but with the necessary attention to personal appearance, any woman can be attractive. However, efficiency must not be sacrificed in favor of appearance. If you need glasses, wear them—discomfort decreases efficiency.

The secretary must look neat and well groomed, all day and every day at the office. She is expected to powder her nose, straighten a stray wisp of hair, and renew her lipstick from time to time to maintain an attractive appearance throughout the business day. This is not to say she should spend the better part of the working day in the powder room—a few seconds here and there should be adequate.

Try to feel well groomed, beautiful, elegant, and rich at the office. And remember that being rich does not necessarily imply that you have money. One millionaire said, "I have been broke, many times, but never poor—being broke means you're out of money, but being poor is a state of mind." If you can't feel rich, feel broke rather than poor—keep your mental attitude in the "rich" bracket and your personality will try to live up to your state of mind.

PROFESSIONALISM FOR THE SECRETARY—NSA AND THE CPS PROGRAM

There are a number of secretarial organizations dedicated to the improvement of secretarial performance, and the largest of these is the National Secretaries Association (International).

Founded in 1943, NSA has a membership of more than 30,000 with chapters in the United States, Puerto Rico, and Canada, and affiliates in foreign countries throughout the world. In the United States, there are local chapters in communities large enough to provide a minimum number of members, and division organizations in each state. International conventions are held each year in selected cities with facilities large enough to accommodate the hundreds of secretaries who attend.

The last full week in April each year is proclaimed locally and nationally as Secretaries Week with Wednesday observed as Secretaries Day. Recognition is given to all secretaries for their service to business, industry, government, the professions, and the community.

NSA defines a secretary as "an executive assistant who possesses a mastery of office skills, who demonstrates the ability to assume responsibility without direct supervision, who exercises initiative and judgment, and who makes decisions within the scope of assigned authority." Dedicated to promoting continuing education for the secretary, NSA has a Research and Educational Foundation and an Educational Consultant. NSA also sponsors the Future Secretaries Association, a program designed to help schools prepare students at the high school, business school, and college level for secretarial careers.

The Institute for Certifying Secretaries, a department of NSA, was established in 1951 to administer the Certified Professional Secretary Examination which has been given annually since then. The Certified Professional Secretary (CPS) rating is achieved by successfully completing a two-day, six-part examination involving environmental relationships in business, business and public policy, economics and management, financial analysis and the mathematics of business, communications and decision making, and office procedures. The Institute is composed of representatives from management, business education, and NSA. The program was established to promote the designation CPS as the recognized standard of proficiency in the secretarial profession. CPS's in the United States, Canada, and Puerto Rico number in the thousands.

If you are not a member of NSA but would like more information on the association, check with your Chamber of Commerce for the address of your local chapter, or write to:

The National Secretaries Association (International)
Suite 910, 2440 Pershing Road
Kansas City, MO   64108

For additional information on the CPS program, contact your local NSA chapter or write to:

Institute for Certifying Secretaries
2440 Pershing Road, Suite G10
Kansas City, MO   64108

The Secretary, a magazine published by NSA, contains articles and information of special interest to secretaries and may be obtained by writing to the Editor and Publishing Manager at the Kansas City office of NSA.

INDEX